To Edw...
for ...ad.

Christmas – 1955

The Secret of

GREATNESS

The Secret of
GREATNESS

by

Reuben K. Youngdahl

FLEMING H. REVELL COMPANY

To my daughter

SUSAN ELIZABETH

CONTENTS

CONTENTS

INTRODUCTION

To BE ASKED to write a foreword for your brother's book is a great stroke of good fortune. It's like being able to talk back to the pulpit from the pew. Of course, I admire my young brother for the miracle church to which he has dedicated himself so completely. I have sat in the pew in his church on numerous occasions and felt strangely warmed by the gospel he has preached. It has rejoiced my heart that he speaks a man's language and knows so well his needs, as is evidenced not only by my personal reactions, but also by the large following of men at those services.

The outsider may think we brothers are poles apart, with Reuben preaching the gospel and myself following the law, but it is my measured opinion that the two must join to make a trunk sturdy enough to support and carry the complicated spread that makes up life today.

I take my cue from my mother. She was very ill at the time I was making a run for a judgeship in Hennepin County, Minnesota. I must have aired my concern for the outcome, because I remember that suddenly she sat bolt upright in the bed and turned with flashing eyes upon me to speak these words: "Luther, I know you are going to get enough votes to win the election, but more important than winning votes is winning souls for Christ." She was teaching me one of life's most important lessons, that is, that every life is a holy calling and only as it fulfills its Creator's purposes and is spent for something that will outlast it can it be deemed successful.

I remember sitting in confirmation class while the minister sketched the story of that great battle between God's hosts and the enemy. The fortunes rose or sagged accordingly as Moses held up his arms in supplication. Naturally there came the point of exhaustion. An expedient was devised. Aaron and Hur were delegated to grasp those arms, and, adding their strength, make certain final victory come. In this day, when a battle (that has every appearance of being Armageddon) is joined between the forces of God and those of evil, it is up to the laymen to step up and grasp the arms of their pastors to promote the Kingdom of God.

Having had a vantage place from which to study American politics, I know how great is the need for Christian laymen in government. Having sat at the table where labor's cause was being arbitrated, I know how urgent is the need for Christian men of good will to join hands for the common good in the field of labor and management. Having seen the callous consciences of some unscrupulous persons in the law enforcement field, I know the necessity for Christian laymen to give leadership in this important area and insist that there be respect for law. Having seen the ridiculed, abused, and maligned members of our social family in mental institutions—these lostlings of society made mute by sickness, guarded walls, and the loss of their civil rights, I know at first hand the demand for Christian laymen to bring humanity into government.

Having reared a family of my own, and also having sat

for years on the bench where our disturbed society sent its flotsam and jetsam, its brokenness for verdict, I feel I can speak to the urgency that men and women everywhere turn to Christ for the Gospel that can give our civilization reprieve. Having attempted to give leadership in an official capacity to a stronger program of human relations, I can stress with deep conviction the necessity of Christians joining hands everywhere to give dignity to every human personality—each created in the image of God. I have a very deep intuition that tells me, America, it is now or never! "Today if ye hear his voice, harden not your hearts."

I earnestly commend this volume and every other word of God that comes to us from our pastors, upon whom I look as guardians of the conscience of our beloved America.

LUTHER W. YOUNGDAHL

Washington, D. C.

11

The Secret of
GREATNESS

CHAPTER I

LIVING ON TIPTOE

OFTEN WE HAVE to stand on tiptoe to lengthen our
reach for something we prize or need. Perhaps it is a treasure far back on the topmost shelf or an apple ripening in
the sun just beyond arm's length. We cannot reach either
unless we stand on tiptoe. So do the prizes in life go to
those who can reach a little higher, last a little longer,
strive a little harder. It is true also of the career of a Christian. Some who take the name never stand on tiptoe to
lengthen their reach. They just shuffle along, eyes on a
level and never looking up or beyond to the horizon. For
them religion is merely a routine of going to church, con-
tributing to its support and expenses, throwing a dollar
into the Community Chest, casting a dime or two into the
hat for alms.

Suppose we try living on tiptoe—millions of us—scan-
ning the field ahead and around us, eager to be of service
to God and to help those who will never be helped unless
we lengthen our reach by standing on tiptoe.

See Jesus, on tiptoe all His life to meet need, to point
the way, to teach, to confound His tormentors. See him
when His enemies sought to snare Him with spurious argument and false charges. They set watch on His words

and conduct, that they might accuse Him of violating some ancient statute, or of crossing some tradition. Recall the time they brought to Him a woman taken in adultery. The law had it that an adulteress must be stoned to death. The men who had the poor wretch in tow decided to confront Jesus with her before carrying out the cruel penalty. They could confound Him, they thought, and then put her to death. If He took the part of the woman He would be setting Himself against the law, thus arrogating to Himself an authority greater than that of Moses. If He consented to her death He would be contradicting His words and deeds of compassion and forgiveness. He would be impaled on one or other of the two horns of the dilemma.

Jesus was equal to the ocassion. He stooped and wrote in the dust. No one to this very day knows what He wrote. Did He put down the secret sins of each of these accusers? And did they blanch, grow fearful at the awesome knowledge of this man? Would He write down their every sin? It seems a plausible explanation, for He finally looked up and said, "He that is without sin among you, let him cast the first stone." And knowing that their lives would be exposed, their souls made naked, they dropped the stones they held ready for the killing, and silently and swiftly made their way from the scene. They could not face Christ and conscience.

Remember also that incident in which the scribes and Pharisees, seeking then also to put Jesus in a quandary asked, "Which commandment is the greatest?" Would the Master brush aside all that God's prophets and His great lawgiver Moses had written, the Ten Commandments? Would Jesus dare to presume to have the last word? With great insight, the lowly Nazarene compressed Ten Commandments into two: "Thou shalt love the Lord thy God with all thy heart, and with all thy soul, and with all thy mind. This is the first and great commandment. And the second is like unto it, Thou shalt love thy neighbor as thyself." In a few words of deep insight our Lord had summed up the Ten Commandments. He gave us the secret of living on tiptoe.

If then you would make the extra effort to carry you to victory in your Christian living, there are two things to watch for. First comes your love to God. For God alone has the answer to your every problem. Secondly, comes your relationship to your fellow man whom you must love as yourself.

With boastful arrogance, Henley's Invictus says, "I am the master of my fate, I am the captain of my soul." Really, now, is anyone sufficient unto himself? Can anyone really build his life entirely by human effort? It is true that many of us merely pretend to need God. When life comes to the clinches, then we try to go our own way rather than seek His help. Isn't that when we really run into trouble?

Let that little boy be our teacher, who riding with a truck driver on a big semi-trailer, begged to be permitted to take over the wheel. They were going down a mountainside with treacherous curves. Its steep incline and the weight of the load put the truck driver's skill to the test in keeping the big vehicle to the road. Still, the boy kept pleading. Finally, the truck driver thought he would teach him a lesson. At an opportune spot he gave the wheel to the boy. Suddenly the boy knew the frightful pull of the truck, and for the first time fully realized his responsibility. He changed his tune, "Take it back, oh, take it back!" he cried.

Many of us are like little boys as we steer the big semi-trailers of our lives. We try to make our way down hill by our own skill. Suddenly, at a turn, we are frightened. We want a hand stronger than our own at the wheel. If only our eyes could be opened wide to see the Master, at our side, offering His practiced hand for the wheel. He says, "I will take the wheel, gladly. I am well acquainted with the machine of your life. Stay with me and we will arrive safely at our destination." It appears to me that the possible explanation of the Christian doctrine of incarnation is born of a collision between God's almighty power and man's self-sufficiency. Move over, man; let go and let God steer.

If we really hunger and thirst after God, be sure of this: He will come over you like a mighty tide. He will sweep into your consciousness and being. Something wonderful will take place; there will be a divine invasion of your life. The Church must have God-possessed souls if it is to arise in this day of world darkness and lead the way out. It is my considered opinion that a twentieth-century Pentecost is breaking over this our day. Signs are accumulating. We are in a harvest time for souls. The more I travel, the more I am convinced of this. The Church has the answer in its Gospel. May God help us to loose it on our world. That sharing cannot be until first we have taken those answers into our own life.

A little blind girl had recovered from an operation to restore her sight. Sitting with her father, she took his hand and looked up into his eyes. A radiant smile broke over her face as she said, "To think that I've had such a daddy all this time and never really knew him!"

Ought we not look adoringly up to God, knowing that

18

He can help us? Is our problem an individual or a community one? He stands ready and able. What a pity to think we have allowed the Father to stand by, and have failed to turn to Him! Are there any who still keep Him waiting for a word?

Let us also consider the earthly relationships. If one hand reaches up to God, the other hand of the Christian must reach out to his fellow man. Our day has benefited greatly by a new translation of the English Bible. It is in the speech of the man in the street. Also, it reflects the last word in scholarship. I sincerely pray that everyone will purchase a copy, that it be found on the desk, the dresser, or the parlor table of everyone belonging to this congregation. Don't use it as an ornament. Take it as a book to live by, as your rule of life. Before another Pentecost can come and the church be reborn, a real movement back to the Word must take place. The first Pentecost came when the disciples sequestered themselves for prayer in the upper room. They must have reminded each other of all the words that Jesus had spoken. The upper-room experience opened the way for the Holy Spirit's coming.

Do you want to live on tiptoe? Do you want to recover from the maladies of sin? Then search the Scriptures, for in them are "the leaves for the healing of the nations." There is no known baccillus that can survive exposure to the sun. To rid ourselves of sin we have but to lift the shutters from our hearts and let in God's sunlight.

Living on tiptoe demands that we keep our human relationships in good repair. We cannot love God without loving our neighbor. Who is our neighbor? The word "neighbor" comes from two words. The first means "near by." The second means "farmer." So, originally "neighbor" meant a "near-by farmer." Today everybody is our neighbor. Boundaries of land and ocean no longer are barriers walling off people from each other.

Accordingly, our love must reach into every part of the world. Hatred never builds. Instead, it smashes and destroys. Only love is constructive. The problem of any man in the whole wide world is really the problem of every one of us. It starts right on our own street. Every neighborhood feud is a microscopic war. We claim to be friends of missions, and support workers in far-away Africa. But if we fail to bestir ourselves for the salvation of the colored neighbor at home we are hypocrites, and our faith is counterfeit. Nor will the world around us pay much attention to a brand of Christianity whose action is inconsistent with its creed. Someone once described a certain type of regular churchgoer as one to whom no one ever listened. Instead, people watched the way he lived the other six days of the week. They asked, "Does he really mean what he professes on Sunday morning?" It isn't going to church that counts. It is going out of church into our week that puts our faith to the acid test.

Is there anyone you dislike? Do you harbor a grudge or nurse a hatred toward any single person? Sit down and write the names of those you hate or dislike on a piece of paper and pray for them before you close your eyes tonight in sleep. I will warrant you that any hatred will melt away. It will be washed completely out of your soul. And when you meet these people speak kindly to them. Isn't that what the Lord Jesus would want you to do? It is that kind of love that our world stands in so great

need of today. Such a love will prompt you to give liber-
ally of your means. Sometimes I wake up at night to hear
the cries of children I have seen in the needy parts of
the world. I know that they are crying for clothing and
food. And, above all else, they are crying for a friendly
hand. There is only one way to still that cry, and that is
for you and me to share our abundance with them. "Thou
shalt love the Lord thy God with all thy heart." If you
do love God, you will love your fellow man.

I once heard a touching story of an awkward, bumbling
soldier. He stumbled over everything. He was the butt
of many jokes. Everybody laughed at him. That is, everyone except an officer, who befriended him. When it was
noted that the boy never so much as said a thank you to
this officer, folks said that it served the officer right. After
all, he ought to know that it does not pay to go out of
your way for an ingrate. One very cold night when the
company was out on bivouac, it was found that only one
blanket apiece had been issued to the men. The officer
was literally stiff with cold and unable to sleep. Suddenly
he felt wrapped in warmth. He had been too miserable
even to bestir himself now to find out what had happened.
Instead, he dozed off to sleep. After several hours, he
awakened to discover that he had on two blankets instead of one. He was mystified. Then he saw the awkward
soldier pacing back and forth in the sharp cold of the
early morning. There was his answer. Several days later,
as a result of the exposure, the boy fell ill and died. The
officer stayed by his side to the end. The smile on the
boy's face as he breathed his last reflected his triumph
—his sacrifice had been worth while. He had repaid the
officer's kindness. Not many of us will be called on to give

up our lives. Yet all of us are called on to spend our lives in worth-while living. Whenever I sing that beautiful stanza of the "Battle Hymn of the Republic" I exercise my editorial liberty to change the phrase, "As He died to make men holy, let us die to make men free." Instead I make it read, "As He died to make men holy, let us live to make men free." It seems the better way to put the thought.

Are you living on tiptoe? Until my dying day I want to keep in memory a prayer I heard one morning in confirmation class. We hold chapel service regularly. This particular morning I said to the confirmation children, "Please pray in your own words today. I want your relationship to God to be that natural. A family needs your help this morning. All of them are believers but a seventeen-year-old boy in that household was called to Heaven just before class began this morning. I would like you to pray on their behalf."

Then one of the girls, shutting her eyes tightly and folding her hands, prayed, "God, we ask that you give the Johnsons the absolute assurance that their son Chuck is happier today than he ever was in his life here." What a lovely faith from the lips of a lovely girl! I said to myself, "Keep to that simple faith, dear children. For then you will always be living on tiptoe!"

CHAPTER II

LIFE'S STOPPING PLACES

Heaven is a prepared place for a prepared people. You cannot live like a devil and expect an angel's reward. On the contrary, heaven must get into our hearts before our hearts can get into heaven. That sense of nearness to God we experience as we grow daily in fellowship with Him will give us in this lifetime a foretaste of the glory that is to come.

It is so very true that today we are building the house we are going to live in tomorrow. It becomes very important, therefore, that we carefully measure our thoughts, words, and deeds. The shoddy materials of selfishness and sin can never build the solid footings of a house which is to endure life's storms and stand until one day it is flooded by heaven's sunshine. Our house must be built on a rock.

If we build it on other than a rock foundation, God, it is by our own deliberate choice. He who does so has said to God, "I am all through. I just do not want anything more to do with you." That is what is meant by the unforgivable sin. A man who keeps saying no to God until he becomes a living no has committed that sin.

All of us have to face many hard things in life. But however bad such experiences can be, we must remember that our Master faced them first. The only cofferdam that knows the full force of the rising flood is the one that did not give way before it. Our victorious Jesus knows the full thrust of every temptation because He never yielded. One of the reasons He came to earth was to prove to us that in following Him we, too, can win victory. We may have our Black Fridays. Yet if we walk through that dark valley with Jesus, we shall find our Easter.

Every Christian prays to be free from the chains of sin. He wants to break the shackles that bind his hand and foot, hinder and stop him on his upward climb to glory. At one time or another every Christian has been down flat. The world taunted him then, saying, "What is the use of being a Christian? Look at the trouble and anxiety you have to go through. What have you gained by stooping under its grim yoke of discipline?" And once he is stopped, once the deadly slough of despond has sucked him in, it is twice as hard to get started again. But what the world does not understand is the courage and inner strength that God gives those who turn and give over to Him the conduct of their lives.

Three things ought to be considered if we want to avoid life's stopping places. First is that we must develop a cheerful philosophy of life and accept the inevitable. We slander God when we say that He is the author of our troubles. That is what the book of Job is about. God gives us the technique to wrest good from the bad. Through His grace we can be victors instead of victims. Nor is God the author of death. This came by the deliberate choice of man to go the way of disobedience and sin. The consequence of that choice was death, the death of the soul through sinning and the eternal death that means separation forever from God. We are remembering Jesus' words, "Fear not them that destroy the body, but fear him that can destroy both body and soul in hell." It is the soul that we are concerned about. Somebody has put it this way: "The devil always votes against you, God always votes for you. That leaves it a tie. You cast the deciding ballot." How true: "Every man decideth which way his soul shall go."

Afflictions and difficulties can weigh us down. We can let them make us or we can let them ruin us. We can reach out and take the hand of God and make our handicaps the very rungs on our ladder to glory.

Again, we can keep life out of stopping places if by faith we dare to attempt the impossible. We are by nature prone to be satisfied with things as they are, especially with ourselves as we are. We do not set our goals high enough. I plead guilty of this in my own ministry. What about you who confess to believe in the might and power of God? If we really believed Jesus' word, "All power is given unto me," what a difference it would make. Every one of us would be staggered and stand back in utter amazement if we could see the tremendous use God might put us to in partnership with Him. A little boy on his first day in kindergarten observed the chairs made to his size and tables just his height. Then he told his teacher, "I don't like kindergarten."

"Why?" asked the teacher.

"There's nothing to grow up to," was the boy's amazing answer.

Here was wisdom beyond his years. Because there is nothing here "to grow up to" explains our spiritual inertia. We have let our dreams and visions die. And on the day

25

our dreams and visions die, that day each of us becomes
a living corpse. What dreams kindled the mind of Jesus!
"Behold, we go up to Jerusalem." He was standing at the
parting of the way when He said that. A grim cross
beckoned at the end of one path. Taking the other road,
He might have found refuge in the hills and in the ob-
scurity of the villages. He deliberately chose the cross.
Starting with only eleven ignorant men, He said, "If I
be lifted up, I will draw all men unto me." The world
traveler is hard put to find a spot on our globe where the
Gospel message has not penetrated. Now what do you
think of that?

It is possible to keep life from its stopping places. The
martyrs succeeded. Again and again handicapped people
have been able to go on because of a stubborn faith. The
blind student on a near-by college campus recounted
to me her valiant story. One day when she was six she
was sitting on the curbstone. Across the street some boys
were playing carelessly with slingshots. Suddenly a stone
struck her. She was blinded in one eye. Because an
operation was delayed, she lost the sight of both eyes.
Totally blind, she cannot even tell the difference between
night and day. She could have given up. People with less
handicaps than hers have done so. Do you and I not
complain and gripe and let our spirits get as low as a
snake's belly in the grass over even trivial things? With
sight denied her, this girl could have become bitter, saying, "God, why do I have to sit here in the darkness?"
Instead she went ahead and put to double use the faculties
that still remained to her.

She learned to type. Facetiously, she said, "The dis-
advantage of handing in your papers typewritten is that

it is easier for your professor to see your mistakes. He cannot read some people's handwriting." She graduated with honors from the high school.

At eighteen she is a freshman at college and keeps abreast with others of her own age. One of her classmates helps her by reading to her from the textbooks. She makes it stick at the first reading. She writes all of her own examinations. A well-adjusted personality, she loves every moment of her campus life. Hers is a beautiful testimony of how when one accepts God's grace one can attempt the impossible. Anything can happen.

If we are going to keep life out of stopping places we must learn in our soul to co-operate with the Eternal. I never tire of reading St. Paul's sermon to the Romans, particularly the second verse of chapter twelve. "Don't let the world around you squeeze you into its own mold, but let God remold your minds from within." When we keep close to God even life's cruelest chapters take on meaning.

A three-year-old girl climbed into her mother's lap. She had been scribbling. The lines seemed to have no meaning. But to the little artist they made a picture. "Mother, what have I drawn?" she asked.

"Well, maybe it is a horse," suggested her mother, "or maybe it is an automobile." You see, the mother could not distinguish what the girl had attempted to draw. The child was irked at her mother's ignorance.

"Oh, mother, can't you see that it is a rose?" she protested.

"Of course, darling," Mother replied apologetically. "Now I see that it is a rose." The daughter was satisfied. After the child was put to bed that night, the mother sat down before the fire to muse something like this: "We scribble along every day and sometimes the lines must seem awfully strange to God. They criss-cross His will; they are blotches on the pages of life. And," she continued, "how can God ever understand what we are trying to make of life?" As she reflected further, she thought of God's great love, of His wondrous patience, and His generous forgiveness. She thought that God in His great Father love interpreted His erring but trusting children's life patterns so: "Yes, I see, you have painted a rose!"

CHAPTER III

THE SECRET OF GREATNESS

WHAT IS THE secret of greatness and who is a truly great man? From the human point of view, the criterion has changed as we have come up through the ages. At one era of civilization a great man was the man who had the most legions. Saul was elected King of Israel because he was powerful and towered above all his fellows. But the centuries have altered that concept. When I was in France I was interested to read of a public opinion poll then being taken. The French people were to select the greatest Frenchman who had ever lived. Because I had occasion to pass frequently through the Arch of Triumph, which commemorates the Napoleonic victories, and to see all the other monuments to war, I naturally thought that the French would have chosen Napoleon. But no! Napoleon had been responsible for the killing of one million people and so he was not chosen the greatest Frenchman. Instead, it was Pasteur, who had worked in his laboratory for the good of humanity, whose whole bent had been to save life instead of destroying it. And, indeed, at least a million lives have been spared because of his scientific research.

There was a time when people said the man with the big bank roll, the man with stocks and bonds, was the greatest man. The secret of greatness was to amass wealth and accumulate all one possibly could for himself. But then came the depression. And some who had lost all their money climbed to the top of tall buildings to fling themselves down headlong, thinking that when they had lost their money they had lost everything worth living for. But as values were sifted men came to realize that wealth is not of the pocketbook but something totally different.

Cecil Rhodes, empire builder of South Africa, was congratulated on his success: "You must be supremely happy!" "Happy!" retorted the fabulously wealthy Rhodes, "Happy! No!" Then he went on to say with a grin that he had spent all of his life piling up wealth, only to find that he had to spend it all, one half on doctors to keep him out of the grave, and the other half on lawyers to keep him out of jail.

What, then, is the secret of greatness? For a time the intellect held the spotlight. We dusted off that old adage, "Knowledge is power." Then the resourceful mind of man uncovered things that could ultimately destroy the race. So again we changed our mind.

I think it is a very hopeful sign that just now many people are going back to the source of life to ask afresh, "What is the secret of greatness?" and "Who is a great man?" God's word has the answer: "Whosoever of you will be the chiefest, shall be servant of all." For "the Son of man came not to be ministered unto, but to minister, and to give his life a ransom for many."

James and John, two of His disciples, had just asked Jesus to guarantee them high places in His kingdom. They wanted to be His prime ministers. So Jesus said to them, "Whosoever of you will be the chiefest, shall be servant of all." And then it was as if He added, "I am going to prove that and thereby show you once and for all the true secret of greatness. Follow in my steps and you will achieve that goal." For He said, "Behold, we go up to Jerusalem." And decisively He turned his back on the comparative safety of the Nazareth country. Jesus could have stayed on there in comparative peace and quiet.

Instead, He chose to go to Jerusalem, the place of danger and the headquarters of His enemies. Resolutely climbing the rocky hills, He went back to face persecution and death by His fellow men. He knew that "he who would be chiefest among them must be servant of all."

I point up just two things as I think in the terms of the secret of true greatness. A man is out there in the midst of life's arena. In this business of Christian living there is a place for every person on God's team. Grandstand sitters are out of place. Soon after the Resurrection Jesus sought out groveling, heavy-hearted Peter, who had denied Him thrice. The disciples had been fishing by the Sea of Galilee at Tiberias, and Jesus appeared to them and summoned them to breakfast on shore. He went up to Peter and said, "Simon, do you love me?" Simon answered, "Yes, Lord, you know that I love you." And immediately Jesus said to Simon, "Feed my sheep," that is, "Go out and prove it, then, by telling others about me."

The Master asks of everyone, "Do you love me?" The very fact that you have taken time from your busy lives to be present here in church indicates to me that you do love God. But He catechizes us as Jesus questioned Peter, "Lovest thou me? Feed my sheep. If there are hungry people, give them to eat. If there are naked and shivering people, clothe them. If anyone is thirsty, give him to drink."

I greatly fear that our churches are thronged with

people who have not done any major wrong. They have not anyone's blood on their hands. They may not even have stolen anything. But they are still sinners for all that, because they are side-line sitters. Like the priest and the Levite, they pass by on the other side when human need confronts them. They are afraid to raise their voices against present-day evils. They would not think of openly persecuting people, yet they share in the guilt of the brothel, the bars, and the slums, simply because they tolerate the existence of these evils under their very eyes. The day has come for the church to exert its influence decisively, to speak up against evil and initiate daring programs against vice and for the relief of need. We cannot be fence sitters when it comes to human need. We must either be decisively for God or we are against Him.

Was the angry Jesus scourging the money-changers from the temple a slip from character? Was He less divine when He gripped the knotted cord than when His hands were pierced and He prayed, "Father, forgive them . . ."? Never! The wrath of Jesus is the righteous indignation He intends followers to show forth. Such anger is not sin. It is compressed prayer turned into a spring stronger than steel, driving us out to where God's people are in need.

Martin Luther said, "When I am angry, I preach well and pray better." Dr. Channing said, "Ordinarily I weigh 120 pounds. But when I am angry I weigh a ton." Our pure food laws are on the books because somebody became angry. Hospitals were once smelly holes filled with raving, pain-wrecked victims until Florence Nightingale got angry. Anger is not the opposite of love. Often it is love's clearest expression. How can Christians stand by while the greedy exploit men's weakness to serve the liquor traffic? Prostitu-

tion thrives only by our sufferance. We are more than a
little short on this anger today.

Stand with Moses and learn how to "be angry and sin
not." In his righteous wrath, he confronted Pharaoh: "Let
my people go." Luther was God's angry man: he exposed
and struck down the sale of indulgences, or forgiveness
of sin. The late Senator Tobey was another. A newspaper
reporter's words ought to cut us like a knife: "Any group
of honest people that gets angry enough can drive out
any crime and make it hot for criminals." Are we Christians angry enough?

The attitude of some so-called Christian can be likened
to the senator described by General Gruenther to me
when I sat with him in his headquarters outside of Paris.
Said the general: "The senator was up for re-election,
so he went back home to mend his political fences. He
asked his friends, 'Well, what is the main issue here-
abouts? I must know what to talk about.' The friend
said, 'It's the squirrel law. Some people are ag'in the
squirrel law. Others want the squirrel law to be enforced.'
So the senator went about and talked to many of his
friends. Finally, he gave a speech and an open forum
discussion followed. The first question he was asked was,
'Senator, how do you stand on the squirrel law?' The senator said, 'Well, fifty per cent of my friends are for it
and the other fifty per cent of my friends are against it,
and I want you people to know that I am for my friends!' "
Well, this sleazy senator thought that by taking a stand
like that he had circumvented the hot seat. Elections,
however, are not the same as judgment day.

No one ever really gets by with that sort of side-stepping
so far as God is concerned. Every person has a responsi-

bility, regardless of how limited his talents or means may be. He has been put in life's arena to do the particular task that God assigned him. And if he fails God it will forever be left undone. I say that the call to serve comes to you regardless of your background or talent.

I often think of some African Christians I met. I visited them in their *bomas*. A *boma* is a defensive enclosure in which are the huts of the villagers so built as to form a wall, which is surrounded by another wall, of sticks and mud. On both sides is bare earth so trampled by many feet that not even a wisp of grass or weed can be seen. During the rainy season it gets muddy, and during the dry season very dusty.

There is one hut for each family. Several women might be married to the same man, for many African natives practice polygamy. This particular *boma* was one in which the house father was possessed of five wives, each of whom was provided with a little mud hut in which she could live with her own children. The men live together. This division of families extends even to mealtime, for men, women, and children eat in separate huts. So when it comes to establishing a Christian congregation, it is very difficult to get any concept of family devotions across because of the complicated situation.

At night the villagers bring the cattle in through the gate to the mud corral in the center of the *boma*. Otherwise the wild animals, numerous in this area, would prey on the cattle. So the villagers and their animals live together in this mud enclosure.

The huts have only mud floors. There are no dishes at all from which to eat. The diet consists largely of a little porridge. "Well," you say, "they have cattle. Then why don't

34

they kill them and get some money?" Our missionaries have urged them to sell some of their cattle and put the money in the bank. But the native reasons, "Money in the bank doesn't get calves." You see, his wealth is measured in cattle. So there he lives, surrounded by his gaunt cattle.

Well, something happens when that African gets converted, and many are converted, for I talked to many of them. I talked to Mr. Neassi, for example. His diet consists mostly of a little porridge. He has no bed to sleep on, only a dirty old mat laid in the mud. He could not even imagine the conveniences we take so for granted here in America. And yet, proportionately, he is giving a lot more money than I am giving in order to build a little mission chapel over there in the African bush. Of course, it will not ever be as beautiful as our stately cathedral church. But it will be holy ground, because the Gospel will be preached there. Mr. Neassi is making tremendous sacrifices for it. "Why do you do it?" I asked him through my interpreter. He said, "My people! I want that more of my people shall get to know the Light of the world. I want that Light to take away the darkness in the hearts of my people." You see, you do not have to possess very much of this world's goods in order to participate helpfully in this far-away field.

My other contention, and this is a most significant one, is that a truly great person not only gives what he can, but keeps in touch with Infinite power. I do not believe that any person can be great apart from God. For God is the sum total of all greatness. Every one of us has the privilege of living every day and every moment of life in His presence. It is His love that would persuade us to help build His world.

35

Theodore Roosevelt once read a book by Jacob Reiss entitled, *How The Other Half Lives.* The book was concerned with the terrible slum conditions of New York City. Mr. Roosevelt was so impressed with the book that he decided to call on the author. When he called, Mr. Reiss was not at home. Mr. Roosevelt left this little note: "Dear Mr. Reiss: I have read your book and I have come to help."

It is my prayer that during the Lenten days we read God's Book regularly, so that when Easter comes every one of us may in spirit lay on God's altar a pledge of reconsecration, and say in our hearts, "God, I have read your Book. I have taken note of your plan to build up brotherhood in this world and to establish peace in the hearts of men. I have come to help. I want to be busy feeding your sheep."

I am not so foolish as to believe that by the simple persuasion of my preaching anyone would ever give himself to greater consecration. If that were in any way dependent on me, nothing whatever could come of it. Nor would I attempt to frighten any of you into being a Christian by preaching hell fire and damnation, and so drive you by fear to give your lives to God's service. I do not believe at all in that kind of preaching. I believe hell's hottest fire will be the torment of knowing that you are forever separated from God by your own negligence. That fire has already begun to burn within you here. It burns there in your soul because your conscience tells you that you are doing what you know you ought not be doing. Instead, with God's grace and mercy, I shall attempt to paint for you, during the Lenten season, a picture of God's great, loving heart. And I would hope and pray that by the compassion of your dying Saviour you may

be compelled to do something for Him while yet there
is time.

Let me conclude with this story. There was a boy who
was very much a problem child. His parents tried to
discipline him into being good. They whipped him and
they spanked him. You see, they used what I would term
the negative approach, which has driven so many people
away from religion. The more they tried to discipline the
boy and condemn him, the worse he became.

Now, the youngster had a cute little puppy. One day
this problem child decided he wanted to teach his dog
some tricks. But Fido only cocked his head and wagged
his tail or just barked. Finally, in the anger of his frustra-
tion, this problem child kicked the dog viciously in the
groin. The puppy tumbled over and lay inert beside him.
At last, the puppy lifted his bruised body and got to his
feet well enough to crawl over to his master and to lick
his hand. The boy broke down in tears. Where discipline
had failed to help him, suffering love had succeeded. It
broke his heart.

I shall ask God to give me grace to hold before your
eyes the broken body of our Saviour on Calvary's tree.
Why did he die? Not for His sins, but for your sins and
mine. I will add the prayer that you may be compelled by
the compassion of Jesus to give your life to Him. The
Master is come and calleth for you!

CHAPTER IV

REAL LIVING

Down A NARROW street in Jerusalem one day walked a man carrying a mattress underneath his arm. You may object, saying, How could a man carry a mattress under his arm? My answer is simple. In that distant land, in that far-away day, the people did not have inner-spring mattresses. (And they do not have them even today.) Their mattress was just a little straw pad. Some were not fortunate enough to have even that. It can be truthfully said that the majority of folks in our world must go without a straw pad for a bed. It was not, then, so strange that a man should be walking along the street with a mattress. Yet this particular man was a sight to behold. Everybody knew him to be the invalid who for thirty-eight years had never once left his pallet.

Let us go back into that man's life. Surrounding the city of Jerusalem was a big stone wall. To enter the ancient city one had to go through one of its several gates. Beside what was known as the "sheep gate" was a reservoir of water. At certain times, because of hidden springs the water would be disturbed. It was believed that if one could get into the water at the time it was being roiled he would be healed of any disease or handicap. And so it

38

came about that alongside this pool of water camped a number of sorely afflicted and crippled people. Can you not see them, with their festering sores, or ulcerated limbs? I suppose still others, deaf, blind, and crippled were led there daily by friends, that they might be near at the moment of the miracle.

Our man had been ailing for thirty-eight years. And for that same number of years he had lain there at the side of the pool hard by the sheep gate. A considerable traffic went in and out that gate. And so to many this man was as familiar a landmark as the gate itself. On a certain day Jesus, seeing this unfortunate man lying forsaken and sad on his little pad, turned and spoke to him. He asked the paralytic what must have seemed a perfectly ridiculous question. For He asked, "Do you want to get well?" The man answered, perhaps something like this: "Of course, I want to get well. But I am a cripple, and when the waters get turbulent everyone else gets in there ahead of me. I haven't anybody to carry my crippled body to be dipped in the water at the right moment. That is why I am still lying here, a hopeless man after these thirty-eight years."

To this wretched man Jesus gave the command: "Arise, take up your bed and walk." And at Christ's command the power of God entered into this paralyzed man. Then and there a miracle happened. The man arose, and, at Jesus' word took up his bed and started for home. That is why we see him walking on the streets of Jerusalem with his mattress under his arm.

A very significant fact in this story is that all this happened on the Sabbath day. It was against the Sabbath law, for the strict interpretation was that no work, not even the work of healing, might be done on that day. So, naturally, when the scribes and religious leaders saw this man walking they sensed that a miracle had taken place. They asked him, "When did it happen?"

He said, "A man, a strange man, healed me. He did it by His word."

They asked for the healer's name, but the man did not know. Searching through the city streets, our healed cripple at last was able to point Jesus out to his questioners. Now they were face to face with Jesus.

The conversation that followed gives me the point for reflection. These misguided religious leaders of the Jews said something like this to Jesus: "Don't you know that it is against the law to heal on the Sabbath day?" Imagine it! They would have delayed the man's healing, given him one more of those endless days of misery and affliction, just to stick to the letter of a law. They had lost sight of the spirit of the law. With intense feeling Jesus turned to them, and I think He said something like this: "You really don't know what living is. Your religion is nothing but a set of do's and don'ts. Because of it you bury faith, with its wonderful freedom and power, in ritual and legalism. We need this word today if we are to live on tiptoe and really live. There are people who have the mistaken notion that if you are religious you are a fanatic, at least peculiar. To live up to their idea of a Christian is to be baptized in vinegar. A long face is associated with praying. One Sunday morning our choir began processing. Just as they were about to step into the church their director said, "Smile, be happy in your singing." That is the word for every Christian. Once I met a girl looking especially glum on a lovely day. I said to her, "Why not smile?" She said, "I can't. Our high school lost a football game Friday night." I am convinced a lot of people let the trivia of life rob them of its gladness. They think of little goals instead of the great good that God has crowded into their lives.

Every one of us has one thing in common, whether we be rich or poor, educated or uneducated. To each of us has been given a life from the hand of God. Some people will say that is good. Others will say that is bad. The cynic says, "Life is just a long headache on a long street, a jail sentence for the crime of being born, a joke that has ceased to be funny." The wise philosopher has this answer: "Life can be abundant, life can be wonderful, life can be thrilling." Which do you want your life to be? Life can be either bad or good. It is up to us. Each of us determines the direction his life is to take. The unhappy religious leaders who badgered Jesus were blind to the good in life. We can be just as blind unless we find life's wonderful dimensions. Failing in this, we can live lives that are cribbed, cabined, and confined. You ask: What are these dimensions? I propose to share them with you.

If life is to be lived after God's pattern there must be the dimension of length. I am not concerned merely with the span of years that will be given us to spend here on the earth. Science has made it possible for man to live longer than ever before. It hardly seems believable that in the sixteenth century the average life expectancy was only twenty years. Today each of us can expect to live sixty-eight years. Just recently science announced that it will add eleven more years to the span. And yet, even at its very longest, life in Scripture's descriptive phrases is but a fleeting shadow, a tale that is soon told. What a sobering thought! Accordingly, we ought to make the most out of this one life we have. We ought to live all the years we have.

Two people have proved to me beyond all peradventure

that length of life is not the important criterion. Who was the oldest man in recorded history? Some of us can be pretty stupid when it comes to Bible knowledge. But is there anyone here who would not be able to give as an answer to this question, the name Methuselah? Maybe you could add also how long he lived. But I challenge anyone here to recall anything written concerning his life. All that Scripture says about him is, "And the days of his years were 969 years." No book ever described his life. Only his name and his span of years are left to us on the pages of history.

Now take just one other person in sacred history. His name is Jesus Christ. He lived only thirty-three years. But what other human ever put as much content into his life, however long, as Jesus packed into those thirty-odd years.

The last words Bishop Quayle uttered just before he died are meaningful. He was stricken at sixty-two by a heart attack while he was preaching. In two swift weeks his life was ebbing. When he was slipping away someone asked, "Bishop Quayle, why do you suppose God is calling you away so soon?"

His face lit up with a smile as he said, "I believe God is telling me that length of days is not as important as our purpose in life. He made it clear that for me this meant to live well, to love God and our friends, and just be glad!" Length of life can be an important dimension only as we live to the fullest, and are glad all the days of our years. These will come only when we add to the span of our earthly years the dimension of eternity. When we are assured that real life beckons just behind the rim of tomorrow, only then can we keep a song in our hearts.

I do not expect to change so much after reaching Heaven as to be beyond recognition. I expect to be myself there in glory. I await with breathless anticipation for life's greatest miracle, being changed into God's image and finding release from the stain and heartache of sin. When I go to live with God I expect to be the same person and so be recognized by those I have loved and lost awhile. It is this assurance that a service like this raises up and nourishes in our hearts. To know that just as the river runs to the sea, so our lives must flow into God's boundless eternity is my most valuable possession. I will never barter it away. All the wealth of the world would be but a mess of pottage compared to this priceless pearl.

There is yet another dimension of life, breadth. Its length gives me courage to face whatever may come. In the teeth of life's worst storm I can calmly say: "I know that my Redeemer liveth." Death unlooses earth's halter, freeing me to be with Him forever. Besides length, we need the dimension of breadth. The happiest people are those who have a broad understanding of other's problems. Their sympathies and interests are wider than the boundaries of their own life. They are extroverts with an outgoing love for their fellow men. Far too many of us live petty lives. Because our memories are so short we must have it repeated again and again that the basic sin of our lives is selfishness. Go back again and take a closer look at Jesus Christ. Look full at His wonderful life. He holds out a key for us. Whenever I hear Americans grumbling that we have to carry the whole world on our shoulders and give and give and give again that others may have the where-with-all, I think, for shame! When will we learn that unless we share our abundance we can lose even our necessities? Look again at Jesus. He gave His all to others.

Is this not just the word we Americans need to hear? We have been God's privileged family. We need to know that every man in this world is brother to us, regardless of his birth,.breeding, or bank account. We had better have a heart for our neighbor. Atomic power is not ours alone. The hand we snub may well have the finger that will pull the trigger that will release the bomb that will leave our country a shambles like Hiroshima. Let us keep in mind that the second dimension of life is "Others." When I walk out into life to live unselfishly for others then for me real life has just begun. When people roll up their sleeves and get into church work without thought of pay, they are really living. It is a joy forever to see some of you go back to your offices with that spirit and make an adventure for Jesus Christ of your relationships with your fellow workers. That is real living; it is living on tiptoe.

There is still another dimension belonging to a life that is on tiptoe. It is the dimension of depth. It is just as important as length or breadth. If we are only pitching a tent foundations are not so important. You can pitch a tent anywhere, but if it is a skyscraper that we are building we had better go deep and be sure that our footings are on solid rock. If this life is our only concern we would not have to be so squeamish, but if we live forever and if it is true that we are building today the house that we must live in tomorrow, foundations are of supreme importance. New York is the tallest city in the world. It is built on an outcropping of rock called Manhattan. Tokyo does not have a single building over five stories tall. It is built on an island of sand. It is what is beneath you that makes the difference.

When I saw the Rockies for the first time I pointed to what I later learned was only a foothill and asked my friend, "Isn't that the tallest peak of all?" He answered, "No! Climb that peak and just beyond you will see a taller one. Climb that taller peak and one still taller beckons behind it."

I thought how much like life. Sometimes I catch myself saying, How wonderful can it be? Then something still more glorious happens the next day. The previous day's joy is like a candle compared to the sun. Scripture puts it beautifully, "We go from glory to glory." God has greater surprises around the corner. But none can compare to the dawn of the day spoken of in these words: "Eye hath not seen, nor ear heard, neither have entered into the heart of man, the things which God hath prepared for them that love him."

A fourth dimension there must be before life is complete. It is height. These four must always be together: length, or eternity; width, the hand reached out in love to everyone; depth, the foundations of God; and height, ever looking up. Life so easily becomes fractional. There is much sin and sadness in what we read and hear and see these days. It all says to us: "Look down!" We become depressed, cynical, and weighed down. We are kept from being the person God meant us to be. Even active, hardworking Christians can compromise by their living the faith they profess with their lips. But God says to us, "Look up and really know what life can be!" You may say, "It is easy enough for you to stand up there in the pulpit and tell us this. But what have you to give to us who are down here in the muck and mire of things, where people are sinning with all the stops out?" I have something. That something is, Someone wonderful beyond degree! He is Jesus Christ. He never fails.

Recently I received a wonderful letter from a friend who has been a continuing inspiration to me. He related that one Sunday, while walking down the aisle of his church, he chanced to look up and see the figure of Jesus in the stained-glass window. At that moment a wonderful assurance was borne in on his soul the like of which he had never known before. His heart became strangely warm with the thought of Jesus' love. He realized fully for the first time that Jesus had taken his (my friend's) place on the cross and now held out in His pierced hands the precious gift of forgiveness of sins. He went on to say that ever since that day, every time he walks that center aisle he looks up to that picture and breathes a prayer that his faith be kept firm and his love warm. It is his lift for the week. I have found again in his experience my life motto: I commend it to each of you: "Look up and live!" Jesus never fails!

CHAPTER V

POWER TO RESIST

CAN ANY PAIN be more piercing than anguish or remorse? Over and over again, burdened people coming to my study say things like this: "If only I hadn't done it!" "If only I'd had the courage to hold out against the temptation!" "If I could only live those few moments over again, how different it would all be!" Haven't we all uttered similar expressions? Physical pain is welcome relief to those who know remorse. Man truly "is wonderfully and fearfully made." He is a split personality and there is constant war between these two natures. The mere fact of becoming a Christian does not end that war. On the contrary, the closer we come to God, the harder the devil presses his attack to win us to his side.

Plato likened man's dual nature to two horses, a black and a white. They constantly pull against each other. Scripture talks about the old man of sin and the new, born-again man with the Christ nature. It all counts up to this: each of us has a capacity for evil or for good. Each man decides which is to have the upper hand. Here is some descriptive symbolism. I can clench my hand and do harm with my fist. I can open my hand and use it in Christian service, and offer to every one the warm handclasp of friendship. The battle between these two natures lasts through life.

Let us try to imagine Peter's feelings as he was warming his hands in the courtyard of the High Priest among Jesus' enemies. Peter had lived for three years in closest fellowship with Jesus. He had been eyewitness to most of the miracles crammed into that brief span. He had seen the blind receive sight, the lame walk, the dead given back to the startled embrace of their loved ones. He had listened to Jesus' wonderful words of life. But in the crucial hour when Jesus was on trial for His life, Peter denied his Lord. Around the fire he joined the flunkies whose rough hands had bound and led Jesus captive. Peter's Galilean accent gave him away. Suddenly a finger was pointed at him and he was asked, "You are one of this man's disciples, aren't you?" Peter showed the white feather. Instead of standing by Jesus, he swore by an oath that never before had he seen Jesus and never had known Him. How different this Peter from the post-Resurrection Peter ready at any price to travel up and down the dusty highways to proclaim his Lord! Tradition tells us that when at last he was led out for execution Peter begged to be hung head down because he deemed himself unworthy to be crucified in like position as was his Lord. And before we judge the first Peter too harshly let us think of the many opportunities for witness we have let slip by because we were ashamed to be counted as one of Christ's. We hid our light under a bushel.

The beginning of hopeful living is repentance. It is faith's initial step. And it takes a heap of courage to make a clean breast of sin. Although Peter had momentarily lost his courage, he recovered his moral balance when he

48

caught sight of Jesus being led from Ananias to Caiaphas. That one look made him turn and run out into the night to weep bitterly. And so Peter kept the faith. Judas looked, too, but only into his own miserable heart. And Judas suffered bankruptcy of both courage and faith and went out and hanged himself over Hinnom's rocky gorge. Why will we repeat that tragic end? Why is it so difficult to humble ourselves and turn to God and say, "God, I've botched things up. I'm sorry"? Why should it be so hard to say, "I'm sorry"? How many heartaches would we be spared, how many broken homes mended if only we could swallow our pride and say, "I'm sorry"! Arguments would never reach the breaking stage if one of the parties would be courageous enough to admit he might be wrong.

Peter lights the way for us. He had a godly sorrow that worked repentance. And after a little talk with Jesus by the Sea of Gennesaret, Peter was ready to write a chapter of unfaltering apostleship. He lived his repentance. One day a little boy came to his mother and said, "Mother, I am sorry." She kept an eye on him for a bit, then turned to say to him, "Sonny, I don't think you are really sorry." With a show of hurt feeling the boy said, "Mother, how can you say a thing like that?" Said the mother, "Because you weren't sorry enough to quit, my son." When we quit sin and live a changed life we prove the genuineness of our repentance.

When he was asked, "Why do you always go to So-and-so's church?" a great psychiatrist answered: "He never preaches a sermon without holding out the forgiveness of sins." This is the heart of my gospel. And since no one who lives can truthfully stand before God and say, "At least, I haven't sinned," the great boon I hold up today is one every soul needs. However far we have gone astray, God is pleading with us now to come home. The terrific increase in mental ill health points up my charge that people are trampling underfoot the free and full forgiveness God offers us. Once we boldly accept God's gift we can be happy in its assurance. A sinful past can no longer taunt us. Instead, ransomed, healed, restored, forgiven, we can joyfully greet each new day. So great is God's love in Christ.

A key to this kind of life has been put into the hands of each of us. The key is repentance and when we stop our futile trying long enough to let God's Holy Spirit work in our hearts just so soon will God's mighty arms enfold us. I do not shut my eyes to the devastation sin wreaks in a life. I want, rather, to put the spotlight on God's all-embracing love. "Though your sins be as scarlet, they shall be as wool" is His promise.

After repentance comes courage. God is faithful. He stands ready to give help against every temptation. No one ever need remain in the wallow of remorse. "Put on the whole armor of God, and you may be able to stand against the wiles of the devil," Scripture tells us.

There are simple techniques to follow if we would be victorious. Peter blundered because he made two mistakes. He followed Jesus "afar off," and then he joined himself to the company of Jesus' enemies at the fire.

Our church is busy erecting a Christian education building. We willingly make the sacrifices involved in the hope of keeping our children close to Jesus through Christian nurturing. We hope also to provide a place for wholesome companionship. If we succeed in these aims we need have no fear of the kind of adults they will become. We know that if parents continue beating the path to God's house, their children will follow, and a real contribution to the solution of the problem of juvenile delinquency will have been made. In the final analysis child delinquency is rooted in parent delinquency. I am as sure of this as I am of God's love, that families that read God's Word and pray together stay together. Not even the devil's fiercest assault can touch them.

Often when we get in trouble we blame it on God. We try all the techniques of self-help only to have them fail us one by one.

Have you stood as I have, fumbling for the coin slot in a parking meter? There must be a thousand different makes of parking meters. No two coin slots are in the same place. One day, being in a hurry, I searched furiously for the slot. In desperation, I was about to give up, when I decided to read the directions. Then it was easy. Here is a lesson. Usually we wait until everything else fails before we read directions. Why will we not remember to read the directions God has given us in His Word before we are tempted?

After courage comes witnessing. God give us courage, not only to repent, but to stand up and be counted for Him. What a chance Peter muffed to stand up among Jesus' enemies and say, "Look, everyone, I am one of His followers. Let me but tell you how wonderful He is, and you will follow Him, too." Every day brings a similar chance to every one of us. When we compromise our faith by sinning we do but drive fresh nails into Jesus' hands and feet and thrust anew the spear into His side. Christ is crucified again before a thoughtless world. May it not be true that thousands have gone over to Communism only because they had no proof that anyone loved or cared for them?

"God! that I was privileged to live in such a day!" was Augustine's exultant shout centuries ago. Surely the Christian Church now faces one of the world's greatest hours of opportunity. Let us not forget the miserable people behind the Iron Curtain. The last thing they really want is to be slaves of a Godless Communism. Can you strike down guns with bare hands? Yet that is what they did in East Berlin June 17, 1953. And because of it thousands have been purged. And still they go to church in greater numbers there than do those in any place in free Europe, and at the price of being sent to the salt mines or off to Siberia. Will we wait until after catastrophe has struck before using and appreciating our freedom of religion?

A soldier boy tells the story of a leper woman in Okinawa. She had sores all over her body and only stubs for hands and feet. Yet, he says, she was the smilingest and most cheerful person he had ever met. He asked her, "How can you be so happy?" She answered, "I am a Christian. Should I be anything but happy?" Being the child of a King, she knew herself to be rich beyond anything the world could offer.

I often think of the heroic chapter of martyrdom being written by a band of 408 native Kikuyu Christians in Kenya, East Africa. They do not live their brand of Christianity behind a stout protective shield, but out in the midst of fierce, blood-lusting Mau Maus. Their bold witness to faith seems only to call forth one atrocity after another. And yet no one of them thinks to tear off the badge that in native language attests: "I am a Christian." How their example ought to brace our knocking knees as we mingle with the crowd in daily social intercourse. What a power the Christian community would know if in America we had that brand of bold witness.

Again I remember a little band of lepers I saw in M'Kalama, deep in Africa. I salute them now in my heart. Their courage to give steady witness to their faith in the face of their affliction touches me to the quick. The divine service I attended there was about to close. Already it was past noon. Although the sun poured through the window none of them could see. Leprosy had robbed them of sight. What a pitiful band of worshipers! Some seemed to have lost all resemblance to the human form. The service closed with the singing of two hymns in Swahili. I quickly recognized them by their melodies. Would that in repeating these lines I could put the haunting pleading these people poured into their singing: "Pass me not, O gentle Saviour, hear my tender cry; while on others Thou art calling, do not pass me by!" Then followed immediately the closing hymn. These blind folks now sang: "Sun of my soul, Thou Saviour dear, it is not night if Thou art near!"

All the truth we know in Christ is in those two lines. Carry it home in your hearts and live by it.

CHAPTER VI

LIFE'S MOST GLORIOUS HOUR

I CAN NEVER forget a fishing trip of years ago. We launched our boats on Rainy Lake in northern Minnesota and went through Namakin and Kabetogama and so back again into Rainy, a beautiful chain of lakes in Minnesota's northland canoe country. A guide and several others were in our party. As we made ready to launch the boat I noticed two motors among our gear—the large twenty-five-horse-power motor fastened on the stern, and the smaller, a two-and-one-half-horse-power motor, lying on the bottom of the boat, which was a long bateau patterned after those of the early French fur traders. Our guide was asked, "Why two motors?"

He said, "We are going into uninhabited country, as you will soon see for yourself." And, indeed, it was difficult even to spot a place along the rocky shore to land these boats with safety. The guide added, "Those of us who travel much in this country know that in case something should happen to the twenty-five-horse-power motor we must have an auxiliary engine with which to return to camp."

He was a prophet, because that huge twenty-five-horse-power motor suddenly developed a cough on the way home and died. Except for the little auxiliary motor, we would have been completely stranded miles away from camp that night. The huge motor which had brought us along so swiftly with rhythmic purr now was only a baffling array of parts from which life had fled. The boat which had streaked so swiftly through the water was drifting in circles. But we did get back, thanks to the tiny motor.

When I have been called on to face life's sudden upsets with people, I have often thought of that day. God has given us a vast capacity for living. Yet we limp along, using only the tiny auxiliary motor of life, our own feeble human effort. We do not give even so much as a second look at that powerful motor that could send us along life's way with the use of only a tiny fraction of its potential.

In all humility, I like to believe that you have noticed one name held above all others in my preaching. It is Christ alone who can take people's lives out of the realm of fractions and make every one of us a complete entity in His work. All of us are just fractions of what we could be only because we fail to utilize the unlimited potential and resources God has made available. God never intended that any life should limp along. We either go ahead or fall back. Life is never at a standstill. It should be an ever-enlarging experience.

One story stubbornly keeps place in my memory. It is of a minister who on meeting a little boy one day asked, "Sonny boy, who made you?"

"Well, to tell you the truth," the little boy replied, "I ain't done yet."

That sharp answer contains a very wise bit of philosophy. The lad realized that he was still being made. He was growing up. The longer he lived, the more opportunity life would give him. So it should be for every one of us—no matter what be the days of our years. Life can be ever so much more wonderful if we sincerely believe in God, who doeth all things well. He gives grace and glory on an ever-increasing scale as we open to Him our lives and our souls and our minds.

In St. John's gospel our Master gives us the purpose of His coming into the world. He says, "I have come that ye might have life and that ye might have it more abundantly." Life "more abundantly" means simply that His blessings are daily to grow bigger. Coupled with that verse from St. John is this word, "And from his fullness have we all received, grace upon grace" (John 1:16, RSV).

Surely life's most glorious hour comes when we find Christ. He alone is the door to the glory of life. Religion and philosophy are not to be confused with each other. One can so easily be trapped in an argument when one expounds his philosophy of life. Opposing viewpoints arise at once. There is room for debate. But altogether different is the reality of a personal experience. One either has accepted Christ as the way or rejected Him. George Fox speaks this truth when he says, "There is One, even Jesus Christ, who can speak to thy condition!" A poor Chinese coolie who recently entered a Christian prayer meeting said, "I am a poor, ignorant coolie, but deep in my heart I know now you-can't-speak-it-joy!" He had accepted Jesus' declaration, "I am the way and the truth and the life." "I am the door, by me if any man enter in he shall be saved." Never have I been more convinced of anything than of the truth that happiness is to be found only with Christ.

Three steps are demanded of us if Christ really is to be our all in all. In the first place, we must approach Him with a sincere mind. Since salvation is a matter of life and death and determines one's eternal destiny, here is no matter to be put aside for a "more convenient season." We err, we who think that happiness is to be found in the accumulation of material advantages. Happiness is not a destination. It is something within you, a state of mind, a condition of one's soul. When one comes to know God and the steadying power of faith, one can face anything that comes along. Deep within is a peace that passes understanding.

We have foolishly attempted to make people happy by tickling their funny bone. We have thought we could increase the world's goodness by increasing its goods. We have been building skyscrapers on bungalow foundations only to discover that civilization is tumbling down about us like a house of play blocks. We have had brains to uncover fearful atomic power, but we have failed to give the man who holds the trigger to these powers the kind of heart and spirit that will make him use these powers for good. The Church, with its saving Gospel and worship of the God of love, has the only answer for this hour of crisis.

Second, if Christ is to be our way, then we must approach Him with an expectant mind. "Why doesn't something thrilling ever come my way?" we often ask. May it not be because we have lost the attitude of expectancy from our lives? Read again Jesus' sermon on the mount. Recall that great word: "Ask and ye shall receive; seek and ye shall find; knock and it shall be opened unto you." God's door of prayer is always open. If we knock at that door he stands ready to help. If ever any belief has been proved, this congregation has proved that God answers prayers. It outgrew first one church building and then a second. Then the third literally burst open at the seams, and this year its walls were moved to make room for additional worshipers. People said it could not be done. Yet, pinning their faith on a prayer—answering God and on His great promises, my people found resources beyond their own.

And then, third, to know life's most glorious hour we must approach Christ with an adventuresome mind. Remove daring and adventure from anyone's life and it becomes as dull as dishwater. I recall Kipling's explorer. This intrepid soul was told, "There's no use in going further; 'tis the end of civilization." What did this trail blazer do? He headed his pony up the mountainside. But before his climb was finished, the pony was dead. Yet the man went on, using up his last ounce of strength, for he was now wasted and sick. Drawing on powers beyond himself, he struggled up the granite cliff to the summit. Then he stumbled down the other side until he reached green pastures, where he was enabled to build an empire, to establish a city, to found a brave new world. His courage and faith turned a dead end into a doorway of hope. Suppose Jesus' twelve disciples had said among themselves at Jerusalem, "Let's keep our Gospel to ourselves," and had spread it no farther than the city of Jerusalem and its environs. Suppose they had failed the Master's command to go into all the world. The Gospel would never have reached our forefathers nor come to America. Our mothers, then, might have been doing what I saw heathen mothers do in remote parts of our world, take their lovely God-given children and throw them into crocodile-infested rivers in order to appease a heathen god. You see, no one had shared with them the gospel of saving love. Someone cared enough, thank God, to bring the glad tidings to our forebears. Our churches now stand with wide-open doors and inviting altars. We may worship according to the dictates of our conscience. In training our children our public-school teachers are not bound by the commands of a few at the top of a totalitarian state, but, instead, are free to give the children the truth as it appears to them. I have three children of my own. I love them more dearly than my own life, even as you love your children. I want for them the best teachers possible. But I know that to have them I must be willing to pay a larger price. For our kind of freedom is costly. The cornerstone of freedom is this great word of Jesus: "Ye shall know the truth, and the truth shall make you free." If we build not on that our freedom will be forfeit and slavery will await us all.

Life's most glorious hour comes when we discover that Christ is the power to keep us in the Way. Every church-goer is a silent witness to the fact that he who seeks it will receive help for his living. He knows that to depend on his own puny resources means ultimate bankruptcy of body and soul. But he is also certain that with God's help life can be wonderful. When I was visiting Livingstone, South Africa, I thought naturally of the man for whom the city was named, David Livingstone, the great missionary. He plunged into the abysmal darkness of the African continent to open it to Jesus Christ. On the night of August 14, 1856, he was greatly discouraged. He knew the native chiefs had joined hands against him. They wanted to wreck his missionary program. He sat down and wrote in his diary: "Tonight I am very discouraged. It looks as if the whole program will fail tomorrow because they are out to get me. I feel like giving up." Then, as if adding a postscript, he continued, "I am going to read the Word of God." Here imagine him sitting with his open Bible, reading, perhaps, "All power has been given unto me in heaven and on earth. Go ye therefore, and make disciples of all nations." He must have turned the pages to another favorite passage, a place also heavily underlined in the Bible he used. It was that word of Jesus, "Lo, I am with you always, even unto the end of the world." Closing his Bible Livingstone again opened his diary to add this triumphant afterthought to that day's entry: "Why should I be afraid? God's presence is with me. I rest in His arms; all is well." If you would claim that same presence, your fears, too, will give way to faith. You will have power to face any temptation that besets you. Your life will be hid in God with Christ.

Finally, life's most glorious hour comes when, having discovered Christ the way and Christ the power to live that way, we turn to share this Gospel with other people. It seems contradictory, yet it is true: "He that hath, to him shall be given: and he that hath not, from him shall be taken even that which he hath." That is true about the Gospel. If we fail to share it we lose it for ourselves. Spiritual death is the awful blight on a hoarded Gospel. Even God's love could not be dammed up. "For God so loved the world that he gave his only begotten Son."

You may wonder and say, "Why did God make such a world with its wars, its moral rottenness, its race tensions, and class differences? I could have made a much better world."

Let me answer, "That is just why God put you in this

world. He wants you to help make it better. Now go ahead and do your part."

I do not for one moment believe that hell yawns for the heathen who dies without Christ. My God will not judge them by the same gospel light I know. He will judge them only by the light they received. A great sense of urgency comes to me when I know the present hell which is theirs in living without Christ. Would that all shared this urgency. Would you want to hear this question at the judgment bar: "Why didn't someone tell me about Jesus before?"

On Calvary's cross hung the broken, bleeding body of Jesus, the greatest sacrifice ever made. It was for you. Whether or not you listen to my word is of little importance. But do not pass unheeding the word of your Saviour and mine: "This have I done for you. What will you do for me?" You, too, can have your glorious hour.

CHAPTER VII

BEYOND THE CALL OF DUTY

ONE DAY A business man found a little ragamuffin taking in every detail of his shiny new automobile. The boy said, "Mister, how much did you pay for this car?" The man said, "I really don't know, son." Taken aback, the boy said, "You mean to tell me that this is your car and you don't know how much it cost?" The man said, "That's right. I don't know what it cost." The boy said, "Well, you don't look to be a thief or like anybody who would swipe anything. I can't understand it." Answered the man, "Well, you see, my brother gave me the car." The boy looked again at the shiny new automobile, but he didn't say what you or I would have expected him to say —"I wish I had a brother like that." Instead, he said, "I wish I could be a brother like that!"

That little fellow put his finger on what is the greatest need of all if God's Kingdom is ever to come to our world. Indeed, if we hope to save civilization from self-destruction, there is no other way than to renew the springs of love. Each must learn to go the second mile, be willing to go beyond the call of duty. That is the burden of Jesus' sermon on the mount. When we do more than people expect us to do, then only do we put His ideals into practice and live as He lived. When we are at the place where our deeds say, "I wish I could be a brother like that," we have gone beyond the call of duty.

Let us take inventory of our talents. They may not seem many to us, but they can be ever so significant if we would give them to God. Our little story does not end here. The man then looked thoughtfully at the boy, saying, "Do you want a ride in my car?" Looking at the plush upholstery and then at his ragged clothes, the boy said, "They're a little dirty." "That's all right," said the man. "Don't mind that, sonny." Asked the boy, "Would you mind going by my house and stopping a minute?" The little boy directed the man to his house and ran inside. In a trice he was out again, a little slower now because he was carrying in his arms his crippled brother. "Look, brother," he cried, "look at that shiny new automobile! Some day I hope to buy you a car like that so you can get out and see all of the beautiful things in the store windows that I have been trying to tell you about."

The story ends with the man driving both boys down to the department store and buying the finest toys available for the two unbelievably surprised lads. What these toys cost our kindly business man I do not know. But every dollar spent that day did double duty. They made two lads happy and gave the business man the supreme joy of exemplifying the spirit of Jesus Christ in his living.

What is the distinguishing mark of a Christian? I mean something very different from the obvious external marks of going to church and reading the Bible and praying, important as these are. When I was in Germany one of the great religious leaders told me that when the people neglected church they left a vacuum which Nazism entered and filled. He added, "Go back and warn the people of America of what follows on the heels of abandonment of religion." We are truly grateful that the people of this community are more faithful in attending church than is the average American citizen. No, I refer to the inner qualities of life when I ask, "What are the distinguishing marks of a Christian?"

Some person might well answer, "Optimism is a distinguishing mark of a Christian." True, a Christian is generally optimistic. He knows that it is the long haul that counts. With absolute confidence in God, a Christian challenges a pagan world, saying, "If God be for me, who dares be against me?" He faces life's gravest problems unafraid because his heart joins with his lips in proclaiming—"I believe in God the Father Almighty, Maker of heaven and earth."

But optimism is not the distinguishing mark that I am tracking down just here. Someone else might rise to suggest that generosity or charity is the distinguishing mark of a Christian. We will have to agree that loving sacrifice breathes the spirit of the Master. Any time I think back over the history of this church I marvel at the demonstrations of God's grace it reveals. Never have we put on pressure campaigns to raise money. Besides this, again and again you have filled my hands with generous free-will gifts for schools in Africa, or for good works in India, when I have taken my world travels. Your arms of love have stretched across the ocean to equip and supply hospitals in India and other places. You expected nothing in return. You gave only because you love God and desire to practice charity in your living. Moreover, on checking the books for our youth camp, the Cathedral of the Pines, the other day, I was amazed to discover the thousands of dollars given for that one phase of our church program alone. People sent me checks by mail or quietly put them in my hands, and have not waited for public acknowledgement. A certain family who asked to remain anonymous came to me one day with the largest check ever received for general camp purposes. They said, "Pastor, we want you to know how much joy we have experienced in deciding on this. We were choosing between redecorating our house or giving the money to the camp, and decided to let the decorating job go for the present." Such spirit reflects our Lord's spirit, and is truly a distinguishing mark of a Christian.

Again, patience could be a distinguishing mark of a Christian. It truly goes with being a Christian. When I think of God's patience with me, coming as I must come to Him each day asking for forgiveness of sins, I am overwhelmed that He is still with me. The unnumbered wonderful benefits he gives me despite my sinfulness and failure to prove by my living that I really love Him are beyond my comprehension. Yes, God's unflagging patience spurs me to be patient with my fellow men, and more generous in my judgment.

Jesus puts all this into sharp focus when He says, "It has been said of old, an eye for an eye, and a tooth for a tooth; but I say unto you, Forgive those who hate you and persecute you. And if they ask you to go one mile, go with them two." Would that the searching look that accompanied His words to His disciples when He asked, "What do ye more than others?" was now turned on us. For in that question is found what I want to call the distinguishing mark of a Christian. There are two significant words in it. The first is "do": "what *do* ye more than others?" I underscore it, because too many even among the religious leaders are trying to take the color and fire out of religion. They want to take joy out of the Christian experience. By the way some Christians act you would think they were baptized with vinegar, not with the Holy Spirit. When you ask the average church member what is involved in belonging to church, his answer will be something like this: "You can't do this and you can't do that. Avoid this and the other thing." But that is a caricature of Christianity and what it really means. The Christian way is not a negative way at all. It is something wonderfully positive. "What do ye more than others?" It is love in action. The shortest description of the life of the Master is put in a sentence: "He went about doing good."

The second word in our question which points up the distinguishing mark of a Christian is "more": "What **do** ye *more* than others?" It is something beyond and above the call of duty. Are other people righteous? You are called to be more righteous. Are other people generous? Your generosity should exceed theirs. Do other people work an eight-hour shift at being "little Christs"? Then you are to be on call twenty-four hours a day. A little lad pointing to a cross on the church altar cried, "Look at the big plus sign!" That is the symbol of Christianity. It is putting the "plus" into every deed. One makes all of life a response beyond the call of duty. It is being the brother the little boy wished he could be. I would like to illustrate it with this story.

Emma Quick was a hopeless cripple living in a wheel chair. She would mournfully repeat, "Life has no meaning for me." Then one day her pastor challenged her to teach a Sunday-school class. That Sunday they carried her wheel chair out of the house, and gently lifted her into the car. At church a circle of children formed about her waiting to hear her unfold the lesson. She has been teaching ever since. She is hopeful. She is joyful. She has wide new horizons splashed with the light of sun and stars. Something wonderful has come into her life because she responded to a call to give herself to others, and crawled out of her shell. It was a call beyond the line of duty. And that, my friends, is Christianity "pure and undefiled."

Again, here is a man named Abram Nightingale. He is a minister preaching in a little wooden church. He has served that one parish for twenty-two years. His name has never been in the headlines, but there is glory awaiting him in heaven. Listen, there is a rap on his door. He opens to find a little barefoot girl standing there. "Pastor, do you have a pair of shoes?" she asks. "I want to go to school and I can't go without shoes." He goes to a corner of his room and hunts through a barrel. A church in Connecticut sent him this barrel of cast-off shoes. He finds a pair to fit and the little girl goes on her way singing. There is another rap at the door. A teacher is saying, "I want to give a prize to one of my best students; have you anything for me to give?" He digs into another barrel and finds a book. A church in Illinois sent him this barrel of things to use in any way he might see fit. So a teacher goes singing on her way. There is still another rap at the door. Someone stands there, wasted and gaunt. He is sick. Abram provides him with medicine, and soon locates a doctor. Just so, he keeps constantly giving of himself about twenty-four hours a day. Now, Christianity is like that.

There is Albert Schweitzer. He is ministering out there

in Equatorial French Africa. One day he sits with a native helper named Joseph. Dr. Schweitzer says, "Joseph, sometimes I think a man is a fool to throw his life away helping these raw savages." Joseph turns to him and says, "My friend, maybe he's a fool on earth, but surely not in heaven." Christianity is like that.

My man is Jesus Christ. He died when He was thirty-three. He had a short three-year ministry. Constantly He went about doing good, helping people. They criticized Him, hounded Him constantly, seeking to thwart Him. Finally, they plaited a crown of thorns and crushed it down on his head. Then they nailed Him to a cross. But before He drew His last breath He listened to a penitent thief calling to Him, "Lord, remember me when thou comest into thy kingdom." And Jesus, using a precious last breath on a common criminal, answered, saying, "Today shalt thou be with me in paradise." Christianity is like that. Only as we practice it that way and go beyond the call of duty are we doing God's will and filling out the pattern He intended for our lives. Then we do His will on earth as it is done in heaven.

A youthful camper with about nine summers behind her reflected that spirit not long ago. Each week at this camp an award is given to the outstanding boy camper and to the outstanding girl camper. It is based on their general attitude, on participation in class activities, their reverence at worship service, their sportsmanship on the ball field, and the like. Nobody knows beforehand who is to receive the award. It is kept a very dark secret. The staff confers with the pastor before making the award. This little nine-year-old lassie's name was called at the award dinner. She was greatly surprised, never in all the wide world expecting to get it. She burst into tears and came running up to the head table. Throwing her arms around the pastor, she kissed him and said, "Pastor, there are so many other kids that deserve this award more than I."

Right after supper that night she went alone to the chapel, where she knelt at the altar. There she prayed God that she might always be a good girl and be ever more willing to give than to receive. To show their pleasure at the honor she had brought their group, her cabin mates collected an offering to give her a special treat at the canteen that night. She accepted it, but instead of buying an extra bottle of pop or a couple of candy bars, she dropped the money into the box marked, "Help Build a Bible Camp in Japan." As I went to sleep that night I thanked God for the miracle He can work so early in little lives. I thought, "What a wonderful world this would be if all of us were to follow the example of this little girl and each of us were to go beyond the call of duty!" and as I passed into dreamland I seemed to hear Jesus softly repeating, "Of such is the kingdom of heaven!"

CHAPTER VIII

WHAT MORE COULD YOU WANT?

WHY WORRY? God has promised to take care of everything that He has made, and He will take care of us. I am sure people generally do not believe this. For if they did they would lead happier lives. And that is exactly what God wants for His children. I am persuaded that there is nothing that He wants more for us than that we should be happy in what we are doing. Out of His great storehouse of blessings He stands ready to give us all that we need. Not only does He hold out the blessings of life, but courage and strength to resist temptation.

If we had lived years ago, and had chanced down a little stony road in the Holy Land, we would have come upon a great group of people sitting on the grassy slope of a mountain. If, out of curiosity, we had stopped to join that crowd, as no doubt we could have done, we would have seen a peculiar radiance about the Person speaking to these people. He was the sole reason for the crowd's being there. If we had listened, we would have heard Him draw one example after the other from nature about Him to illustrate His message, for He always preached by illustration. He put His truths in such nice little baskets that they were easily remembered.

Now, Jesus discerned fears in the hearts of these people even as today He uncovers fear in us. In substance, He told these people, "God, who made all things, is my heavenly Father. I have come from Him, and can tell you what God is like. God made the grass, the flowers, the birds, the mountains, the lakes, the rivers, the streams. Moreover, God sustains the breath of life in us. Man was the crowning climax of all God's creation. For He made man in His own image. He breathed His breath into man's soul, and made man the most valuable part of His creation."

Now look about you. Over there are some birds. They do not worry. They do not sow crops, nor yet reap grain. On awakening in the morning, the first thing they do is to sing a song. They do not even know where they are going to get their breakfast.

Or take a look at beautiful flowers. They do not toil, nor do they spin, and yet, for instance, have you ever seen anything as beautiful as a full-blown rose? What causes the seed lodged there in the dark clod to break forth and struggle from the ground into the air and then into view, bringing forth beauty of stalk and bloom, and seed for renewal? It is the power of God.

Now, if God takes care of an insignificant sparrow, if God takes care of a little flower that man tramples underfoot, don't you think that God will take care of you, oh you of little faith? Why worry then? God has promised that He will take care of everything that He has made, and He will take care of you.

Let us look for a moment at man's concerns. They are very real. At some time or another we all come up against problems that we cannot possibly handle in our own strength, for we are living in a complicated day. A statistician figured out that one hundred years ago there were something like seventy-two needs of mankind of which about sixteen were declared to be basic. Today, a hundred years later, there are four hundred and eighty-four needs of mankind, with only approximately ninety-four of them considered basic!

Competition is the life of business, and it is especially strong in today's world. I am keenly aware of some of the temptations that must be faced daily. I know some of the problems that youth run up against. I see all about me homes that are breaking down. I see men, and women too, becoming enslaved by degrading habits. From the depth of their hearts and souls they cry, "Show me a way to be set free."

"If you will but take me at my word," God says, "and sincerely believe on me, I will give you the strength to meet any emergency in life." A man orders a bowl of soup. But, when it is put in front of him he complains to the waitress, "I cannot eat that soup." She asks, "Why, what is wrong with it?" "Nothing is wrong with the soup," the man explains. "I just haven't a spoon."

God has provided abundantly for us. It is up to us then, to use our ingenuity to look for and make use of the things He has given us. Let sunshine and bird song sink deep into our souls. Oh, the sheer joy of living and being a part of this glorious creation which God shares with us all, rich and poor, black and white. Get a spoon and reach out for all of it—yes, and for redemption and the cross and forgiveness of sins and all God's blessings!

A displaced person had so little food for his family that he had to hide it and then ration it out daily. His little seven-year-old girl was so hungry that she crept furtively to the basket in early morning and took a piece of stale bread from it. And for that her father whipped the seven-year-old child at three o'clock in the morning. "If I could feel full just once!" was her piteous complaint.

I am very much aware that in talking about America's abundance today we must frankly face the fact that the blessings are not equally distributed. Nor did God mean that they should be. He meant that individual initiative should play a part. But sometimes circumstances hedge in and thwart even the most resourceful. And here is where sympathy and sharing and Christian generosity make their contribution. God's great plan includes the use of loving hands to pass along His gifts to the needy, among them the displaced persons of the world.

"Oh that I might intimately know Him, even feel His hand touch my life!" was the cry of a new convert.

"Have you ever prayed for that?" asked her counselor.

And when the answer was, "Why, I never thought of that," it was suggested that right there and then they kneel and ask this gift of God.

Shutting her eyes tightly, the new beginner prayed, "Please lay your hand on me, O God."

And as she did she cried, "He did touch me!"

Then after a moment's thoughtful pause she said reflectively, "But, do you know, it was strangely like your hand!"

"It was mine," answered her friend. "Whose hand did you think it would be?" When God wants a hand to do a loving deed He uses the ready hand that is nearest. Let me suggest how everyone can help himself:

A good practice is to take every fear by the scruff of its

neck and drag it out into the open. Line up your fears where you can face them head on. There may be an army of them arrayed against you, but I have found it good therapy to pose the simple question, "If the worst did happen how bad would it be? Is it more than you and God could handle together!" Remember, "One man with God is a majority."

Then repeat this simple verse again and again to yourself: "If God be for me who can dare be against me." And when next an overpowering temptation assails you and you are about to play a coward's part, ready to give in, ask God to perform His good work in you as He did in St. Paul, who said, "We are more than conquerors through him that loved us."

With all my heart and life I believe that God is, and that He cares for me as an individual. I believe that God has a specific plan for my life. I want to make it my life passion to fill out His pattern and know His good and perfect will. If we could all resolve to do this, nothing could ever really overwhelm us.

When we awaken in the morning, let us say, "God is for me." And when we sit down to breakfast, let us add these words to our thank you blessing for food. Wasn't God in the whole process of rain and sun and growth that brought the food to the table?

In the office problems may soon arise which we are incapable of handling alone. Stop and take a moment to say, "God is with me!" You will be amazed at how many different ways God has to help you. You will soon discover that God will help you keep your head clear so that you can avoid the pitfalls of doubt and anxiety and overcome the temptation to be slothful or careless.

And at the end of day let God have His due. Do not carry today's burdens into tomorrow. Slam the door and draw the curtains on them. Say, "God, here is my record, with all its mistakes and heartaches and successes and joys," and God will smile on you in love, forgiving and blotting out every sin. Only then will rest come naturally. It can happen that way. What more could we want than that?

Bombs were bursting about a young pilot flying high over Korea. The lad was mightily afraid. "Suddenly I got hold of myself," he said. "The Twenty-third Psalm that mother had taught me popped into my mind—'The Lord is my shepherd, I shall not want . . .' That cleared my head for decisive action and brought peace and calm to my soul." Against the day of our great need let us make such faith our faith!

A woman who regularly went to church and kept to a certain pew often left little crumpled bits of paper on it. One day, being curious, the sexton flattened out some of them to see what was written on them. He read such things as "Janie sick," "John without a job." Puzzled, he took them to the minister. The next Sunday the pastor asked the woman to stop for a moment in his study. "I don't mean to be inquisitive," he said kindly, "but what do these little slips of paper mean?"

"I read a sign on the streetcar," she explained, "which said, 'Take your troubles to church with you and leave them there,' and so I have been writing them down on little slips of paper and leaving them. It is wonderful the way God has helped me."

"God bless you," exclaimed her minister, "I know that

He will continue to honor such a faith and keep helping you!"

Why worry? God has promised that He will take care of everything He has created, and God is faithful to His word. God Almighty will take care of you!

CHAPTER IX

STARS AFTER STORM

IT WAS CHRISTMAS EVE. Two Minnesota GI's had just completed sentry duty at their station near London. Had they been home here in Minnesota they probably would have gone to their respective churches. But on this particular night they got into a jeep and drove into London. On the way they went by a building with a sign reading, "Queen Anne's Orphanage," and afterwards learned that the parents of the children being cared for here had been killed in a bombing raid. On impulse they stopped and went inside where they found a group of sad-looking children gathered together. And although it was the eve of the day of days for children, there were no Christmas trees, no smiling faces, and no presents. The GI's put together what they had—their pocket knives, their scarfs, stubs of pencils, and a few extra coins, and gave them to these forlorn children.

One of the soldiers saw a little boy sitting in the corner of a room looking especially sad. This blond, blue-eyed boy reminded the GI of his favorite nephew back in Minnesota. He walked over to the boy and smilingly said, "Son, what would you like to have?" And the little boy looked up into the soldier's face and said, "Please, sir, I want to be loved." After having traveled forty thousand miles and visited twenty countries, I am surer than ever before that, "now abideth faith, hope, and love; these three, and the greatest of these is love." The shortest definition of God includes everything: "God is love."

I stood with our consul-general on the shores of the Mediterranean just outside of the city of Beirut and looked at the wreckage of a ship piled up on a rocky reef a little beyond the harbor. Just after the ship struck the reef the passengers got panicky. Word got around that it would be approximately twenty-four hours before a boat could get to it through the mountainous waves, and they were struck with the fear that their ship would break in two. So about sixty of them jumped overboard into the angry waves. Fifteen of them were dashed to pieces on the jagged rocks. I asked the consul, "Why did the ship strike the reefs?" He answered, "The pilot chose the wrong beacon." So, as a result, scores perished in full sight of port. The harbor lights which had been to them like stars to a mariner and given them hope that danger was past now only deepened the tragedy of storm and disaster.

While I was on a plane to Johannesburg, South Africa, one day, the air became exceedingly rough. A violent summer storm was breaking about us, and we headed into a particularly menacing black cloud. Evidently, the pilot was trying to decide whether to go through it or around it. He chose to go around it, and, instead of storm, we found clear weather, blue sky, and, after nightfall, the stars. In the crisis of decision up there in the air, I thought then, as often before and since, "every man decideth which way his soul shall go." Momentous decisions that will shape destiny for generations to come must be made today. I do not wish to give the least suggestion that we face a hopeless future. I believe with all my heart that we stand on what can be the threshold of the world's most glorious hour if only people generally will decide to go God's way.

There are threatening storms over Europe today. I talked with the High Commissioner in his office in Bonn, Germany, a few weeks before the Big Four talks began in Berlin, and I learned, for example, that Europe fears war with Russia much less than we do here in America. Many people are praying and hoping against hope that there will not be another war. Living amidst the ruins of the last war, they do not want to believe that another is in the making. They are convinced that at this moment Russia is in no position to start another war.

That does not mean, however, that the spread of Communism to other countries has been halted. In an election in Italy, for example, the Communists received thirty-seven per cent and the controlling power only forty-one per cent of the votes. It may be argued that it was a protest vote with an anticlerical cast, that is, a vote against the Roman Catholic Church.

Western Germany, on the other hand, is rebuilding with unbelievable vigor. Hamburg was erecting a school a month at the time of my visit. The fortitude of the people after the terrific bombings that leveled their city is perfectly amazing. They are working from early morning until late at night rebuilding their industries and cultivating their farm lands. Russia's policy toward the West had even softened a bit. People from the East zone were permitted to go over into the West zone to visit relatives

79

whom they had not seen for years. One feels a deep pity for these poor, fear-driven people who are being ground under the iron heel of a brutal oppressor. Perhaps, I thought, it is divine judgment against them for not having blocked Hitler's bloody hate programs.

An East Berliner said to me, "Mr. Molotov will probably come to Berlin and talk and talk and talk. And then when he is through he will say, *Niet* or Not yet, and then we will have to go back to our misery." Our State Department was taken completely unaware by the spontaneous uprisings of June 17, 1953, throughout Eastern Germany. It could not understand how people could think of facing soldiers armed with machine guns and cannon-mounted tanks with only bare hands. But the people said, "We would rather have death than slavery." Then you understand why I came back home more grateful than ever to God for being privileged to live in America today!

I was disturbed by the storm clouds with their ugly pattern of hate over Palestine, the very land in which Jesus lived and walked. I visited the little village of Kibya. On October 10, 1953, the Israeli army in force went into this unarmed city under cover of night and massacred over fifty men, women, and children, and left the mutilated bodies lying in the streets. The victims had not even a chance to flee. I saw Arab soldiers, barbed-wire entanglements, and tank traps, and military installations. I heard marching men chant, "Remember Kibya," while they prepared for a new war of revenge. These storm clouds were painfully visible just beyond the fields where angels sang, "Glory to God and peace on earth."

There are storm clouds over East Africa. When I was in Nairobi, I observed the military trying to control the

Mau Mau situation there. Right across the street from me I saw soldiers with drawn bayonets forcing the shop-keepers out for routine examination. If they did not walk fast enough to suit them the soldiers would jab them lightly in the back, tearing their clothes. Machine-gun installations were placed at each corner ready to spray the people if they made a false move. And while I was walking the streets of Nairobi, two Africans from the Kikuyu tribe were shot to death in cold blood. (No one could tell me whether they were innocent or not. I must assume that they were. They hadn't obeyed orders fast enough.) I saw the military line up these Kikuyus for search. Not one in the group I watched but had proper papers. None of them was charged with ever having taken the Mau Mau oath. Apparently it was only a routine examination. To me it seemed as if the soldiers were look-ing for opportunities to show their authority. They made these natives stoop and then stand, stoop again, and stand another spell. While I watched I could see the gleam of hatred in the natives' eyes. And my Kikuyu driver said to me, "I will have nothing to do with the Mau Maus. I don't approve of their policy, but these people are forcing us into something."

British and American authorities declared that the mili-tary could easily bomb these Mau Maus out of the hills. But who will heal the wounds of hate and rebellion such action would leave in those hearts? At Arusha, just outside of Nairobi, I spent the night in a missionary's home. I later learned that the Mau Maus crept within twenty feet of my window. But they did not pause to molest us or do any damage. Instead, they continued to a house about a quarter of a mile from the missionary's home, where they murdered a native Kikuyu family, slashing them to death with their knives because this loyal family had given the police information about the terrorist activities.

There are very black storm clouds over South Africa today. I cannot understand how an ordained minister, Dr. Malan, who until recently headed the government of South Africa, or his reactionary successor, can insist as they do that God created the white race to be a master race. Instead of preaching brotherhood and seeking to get across the idea that all men are created equal in the sight of God and so should have equal opportunity, these leaders have forced the jacket of segregation on South Africa, widened the breach between the races, and stirred up bitterness at this critical time in world history. As an example of the inequalities let me cite the case of a mail carrier. He runs thirty-six miles a day back and forth to a certain village. For his arduous running he gets half a shilling or just seven cents a day in our American money. Think of it! Is there no hope? Yes, I see a star in this storm-darkened sky.

My wonderful friend, Dr. Moll, of Jerusalem, told me about a Christmas Eve service in the fields of Boaz, the same field where the shepherds held watch the night that Jesus was born. This field is about two miles long and one mile wide, and is adjacent to the city of Bethlehem. Dr. Moll says, "It was Christmas Eve in 1953, and I was to preach the sermon at an open-air service on this hillside. What a contrast we saw on every side as we made our way. There were military installations along the road; soldiers armed with guns stood with their fingers on the triggers. We knew that at any moment there could be a blinding flash and the roar of guns. Just one trigger-happy

82

soldier and the battle would be on. At the same time a
storm with thunder and blinding lightning complicated
the scene. It seemed that nature and man were conspiring
together to try to thwart the message of the Prince of
Peace.

"At last I arrived at the shepherds' field. Just as the
service began the curtains of heaven were drawn aside and
first one star appeared and then another and another until
the sky was studded. How could I help being reminded of
that long ago when God pulled aside the canopy of heaven
and sent an angel down a staircase of fleecy clouds to
earth, the angel all the while singing the joyful message of
the birth of Christ the Saviour. I knew then that there was
hope for our world. One had come who would answer
every question and solve every dilemma and open to us
the way to Heaven. It was my Saviour, mighty and able
to save."

In the little village of M'Kalama among the Zulu people
is a leper hospital supported by the mission funds of our
church. We arrived there a day early. The patients had
been told that two visitors were come from America. So
when the bell rang these people came expectantly to the
church in order to meet us and share a service together.
We waited for an hour after the bell, and, sure enough,
the people came streaming in from over the hills and fields,
all dressed in their best clothes. Some of them did not
have toes. Some of them had only stubs for hands. Others
had open, ulcerous sores. Several stood up at the meeting
to bring us greetings. First, the head of the board of the
local congregation spoke. He was followed by the representative of the Women's Society. And, finally, a woman
seventy-six years old who had been converted while she

was at this leper colony spoke. She impressed me deeply. Her hands were stubs, with no fingers at all. She had practically no feet, and was blind from leprosy. Yet she got up to speak. She did not try to come up to the platform, but just stepped into the aisle. She smiled as she said, "I am so happy today. I know that you friends who are with me in church today are happy, too. It is because we have seen these two friends who have come all the way from America. I am blind and cannot see them. But, nevertheless, I want to thank them and ask them to thank their people back home for sending missionaries here to give us a faith to live by. They have put a great joy here in my heart. They have taught me to know that though I cannot see my friends here today, yet I know that one day, by God's grace, I will see them in His House of Many Mansions."

I choked up as she sat down. A well-known verse of one of our hymns kept running through my mind. It was this:

All hail the power of Jesus' name!
Let angels prostrate fall;
Bring forth the royal diadem,
And crown Him, Lord of all.

When nations bring forth the royal diadem and individuals hail the power of Jesus' name, the storms over our world will be past, and God will set out the stars to light us home.

CHAPTER X

ARE YOU READY FOR THE KING?

IT IS ADVENT! Sound reveille! "Awake out of sleep!" "Abound in hope." "The Lord comes, who will bring to light the hidden things." "The Lord is at hand." These are the bugle calls of the four Epistles assigned to these Sundays. The Gospels are even more arousing. Like a much repeated motif in a symphony score is the one persistent call through them all: "Christ is coming soon." It follows that the order of the day must be, "Get ready!"

When is He coming? "At an hour you do not expect," is Scripture's answer. There are some would-be prophets who do violence to this answer and by using the "holy" numerals found in the Book of Revelation figure out formulas to fix the exact date of the Lord's return. We prefer to take God at His word when He says explicitly, "No man knows the hour."

It is sobering to consider that at a specific time Jesus will come again. Then should we look to this event with dread? Indeed, no! Jesus' own word is, "Look up, for your redemption draws nigh." Rather is it a glorious event to be joyfully anticipated. And if we are ready and prepared for His return this will be our mood.

Many people lose so much that God offers merely because they look on Him as One to be called on only in a desperate emergency. They have never tasted of the pure delight of being always on speaking terms with Him and walking daily with Him. They do not know Him well enough to adore Him.

Students know well that there are two ways to prepare for an examination. They can either study every day and gradually learn their lessons so as to be ready at any time for a quiz, or they can stay up the night before to cram for the test. Far preferable is it to be always prepared. Two little girls were talking about a grandmother who was constantly reading her Bible. "Why is she always poring over her Bible?" asked one of the other.

"I guess it is because she is cramming for her final examination," was the reply.

That is the way some people treat life. They do not live in the faith day by day. Consequently they miss God's breath-taking adventure of being followers of Christ every day. To be prepared and ready for His coming at all times is a wonderful way to live. Janie was late at school. Her mother sent this note to the teacher: "Please excuse Janie for being late. Nine o'clock came sooner than we thought." Sooner than we think the glad cry may ring out: "He comes!" But if we are ready, what is there to be afraid of?

What is involved in this wonderful way to live?

It means, first of all, to know and practice a faith fit to live by. We can do one of four things with life. First, we can turn and run away from it as Jonah tried to do. Like Simon Stylites of old, we can climb a high post and take refuge from life's harsh realities. This is obviously very unrealistic. What positive help could we offer from the top of a pillar to those in the muck and mire below?

86

Second, we can join the crowd and cry, "Crucify Him!" Third, we can try to manage life as best we can on our own. Fourth, having learned that the demands of life call for resources beyond our own, we can accept God's proffered help.

When God is invited to go along with us we will have the experience of a certain little boy. He was sent to the basement to fetch the basket containing the day's wash. He was just a wee mite of a boy, but he did want to obey his mother. The clothes were wet and also very heavy. To pick up the basket and carry it upstairs was just more than the little fellow could do. He tried and tried again. Suddenly he felt a presence behind him. Strong arms were lifting with his chubby short ones. Now the basket was nothing at all to carry. You see, his father had joined his strength to his son's. It was all to the boy's credit that he had obeyed and had tried to the utmost of his ability. Accordingly, he fully shared the joy of accomplishment when the basket was delivered to his mother. We are not to sit piously praying to God to get things done. If we pray, believing, we will also present our abilities for God to use. Such praying gets even the impossible done, for God adds His almighty strength to our feeble effort. His strong arms will help ours. His mighty shoulders will be under our burden. Suddenly we reach the top of the stairs and victory is ours.

It works every time. What about the great missionary's slogan: "Ask great things of God, attempt great things for God"? But it is not magic, nor does it come by pushing a button. A faith to live by is a faith that appropriates every gift God offers to all of us. It is a wonderful way to live.

To have a self that is fit to live with is the second key to this wonderful way to live. To be caught in the center of conflicting selves, to be torn by bickering and fightings within until one is tense with strain and all wrong inside, is an experience all of us have known. Good and evil vie for the upper hand. The result is that we are miserable all the time. We cannot be happy either with God's children or in the company of sinners. Trying to set this mess straight by such externals as going to church regularly is only putting a mustard plaster over a malignant tumor to heal it. We must, instead, let God's Holy Spirit apply His therapy. What would you think of a jeweler who would suggest changing a hand or replacing the crystal of a broken watch to make it run again?

You may have friends between whom and yourself you think everything is "sweetness and light." Yet when your back is turned they may stab you with their sharp tongues. But before you judge too harshly or strike back, consider the fact that they may be suffering from an internal conflict. A newspaper clipping in my file sharpens my point: "Never be unkind to anyone, not even a crank. When you are about to crush someone who has annoyed you, look before you strike. For when you see what you are about to do, you will not do it. In attacking a crank you may be striking a wounded animal." Some people are miserable because they do not have a self fit to live with. God being shut out, there is no Almighty hand to throttle evil within or point the way to victorious life.

The haunting lines of our Advent hymn puts it just right: "Thy heart now open wide, bid Christ with thee abide." Once we give room to God's grace and power and our hearts are cleansed from sin by a thoroughgoing repentance, we will experience a spiritual dynamic more than sufficient to carry us through any evil or over the most difficult hurdle in our way.

Many of us are petty and small. We let little irritations upset us. The great English statesman Disraeli said, "Life is too short to be little." At best, we spend three score and ten years, or if by reason of great vigor, four score years, or a few more, on earth. Life is too short to be little, to let a slight or seeming rebuff or someone's aggressive elbowing us out of line give us a heartache. Those who love God have bigger things to be busy with.

It is a wonderful way to live when one has a cause worthy of his effort. What would we think of men who have the creative genius to discover such drugs as sulpha, aureomycin, chloromycetin, penicillin, if they had said, "We are not going to share these discoveries with the world. We intend to keep them for our own families only"? Such selfishness would be beyond describing.

Worse than cancer and worse than any organic diseases that these medicines cure is the disease of sin. The gospel of Christ is sin's only cure. What will those who sit in its hopelessness and darkness think of us if we fail to share Christ with them? Christ is on His way. Sooner than we think the glad cry may ring out: "He comes!" It may be that someone in our own family, someone in our office, or some neighbor may be waiting for the word of hope from us. It could well be that only we could bring them to Christ. The impelling motive back of both foreign and home missions is ever this: "We are debtors."

The history of the Church is only the unraveling of a great informal movement of one person sharing Christ with another. The office, the football field, the street, the school corridor, the home—these are our mission stations, our pulpits. Here we either proclaim or defame the Living Word. More glorious chapters are yet to be written.

With a cause fit to live for as our incentive, what glory beckons just over the rim of tomorrow! Tom Perkins was a wonderful Christian. As he was breathing his last, he seemed to look out through the shutters as he exclaimed, "Glory! Glory! Glory!"

His wife looked out too and commented, "Yes, Tom, it is a glorious sunset. Shall I open the shutters wider to see better?"

"My dear," he replied, "I have seen far, far beyond the sunset!"

Have you got that long look? Do you hear within you "deep calling unto deep," and so are you therefore on tiptoe, eager to know what God may have in store to-morrow? Let us keep our house in order for His return. It is a wonderful, wonderful way to live.

CHAPTER XI

SO MUCH FOR SO LITTLE

ONLY ONE LEPER returned to give thanks. That is
not a very good record, considering the loathsomeness of
the disease and that there were ten who were healed. I
have seen many sick people in my life. I have seen patients
toss restlessly to and fro with raging temperatures. I
have seen young and old stricken with polio. On my travels
I have seen children walking about with running, fly-
infested sores on their hands and feet and on their faces.
I have seen whole communities infected with contagious
disease. I have also seen the arm of love come with vita-
mins and medicines such as penicillin and wipe out disease
from an entire community. I have seen how happy and
hopeful these people become when the cure is effected.
But I know of no disease that depresses me more or that
is more loathsome to me than leprosy.

Ten lepers came to the Great Physician one day. They
were social outcasts. Their families did not want anything
to do with them because they were afraid of this revolting
disease. Cut off from home and opportunity for gainful
employment, lepers were bereft of all hope. People shrank
from them and were impersonal and heartless in all their
dealings with them. But not so the Master. He stopped on

His busy way when He saw them. He even reached out His hands to touch them, and so healed them of the disease.

Can we conceive of what it would mean to return to normal life, with its pleasant social contacts, after having been a hopeless outcast for years? And yet only one of the ten returned to give thanks.

Lest we become too severe in our condemnation of the nine who did not come back, let us give ourselves a hurried examination. We have been afflicted with a disease far worse than leprosy. There is nothing worse than the sin disease, for it separates us from God and cheats us of all things spiritual. But God has not forgotten us. He has reached down with His great arm of love to touch us and heal us of our loathsome disease. Yet how few of us have really given Him thanks with our living. How few of us have given back to God of our means, talents, and time in proportion to what He has given us and continues to give us of His blessings!

We have all faced crucial problems and sudden emergencies. Then we turn to God, saying, "If only you will come with your power and help me God, I promise to love you as I have never loved you before." But the emergency past, we go back to the same rut. When we got well our resolutions to be different were forgotten. We forget the clouds that blotted the sunshine from our lives.

Today as we think of all that God has meant to us and done for us, let us resolve afresh to reconsecrate ourselves to Him. For by giving of our lives in self-forgetting service we show our gratitude.

God gives us so much for so little. In spite of all our

pride in ourselves and in spite of our creative genius, we have such puny strength as compared to the power of God. In some parts of the world spring brings floods, and hundreds and thousands of people's homes may be threatened. Trucks are commandeered and men are conscripted to carry sandbags to build up the river banks. But the mighty force of the rivers ofttimes breaks through man's little dikes as if they were made of reeds. Like that is the puny little power of men compared to God's Almighty power!

One man confidently steers his ship across the Atlantic. He has a record of never failing to reach port. But this time a hurricane strikes the ship and it is powerless against wind and wave. Fatal sickness fells whole communities in spite of marvelous scientific discoveries that help so to alleviate human suffering and cut down the mortality rate. We have prolonged the life span of man. Yet his creative genius has not been able to stop death in its tracks. We are such tiny little creatures when compared to the greatness of God.

And yet God does not detach Himself from us or is indifferent to us. If we but admit our littleness and failures and give ourselves into His hands, God can use our lives for great good, no matter how insignificant they might be in our own eyes.

Some one asks me, "What advantage is there in being a Christian if hardships and troubles must come to all people?" I am reminded of the blacksmith who says, "I take a piece of steel. First, I put it into cold water. Then I put it into the fire. Again I plunge it into cold water. Now I can bend it and shape it. If it is a good piece of steel it has true temper. It can usefully serve where strength and tenacity are demanded. But if I notice that it will not stand the temper or the change from hot to cold I throw it into the scrap pile. It is finally sold for a half a cent a pound." And my blacksmith philosopher continues, "Now, God does that with my life. He puts it into the fires of temptation and trial and burdens, and then He plunges it into the cold water of discouragement. So He tempers us to make us into something useful. The only prayer I keep praying is this, "God, please don't throw me into the scrap pile." If we sincerely try to find His purpose for us in whatever happens in our life we will never find ourselves in the scrap pile.

God offers so much help and so much hope to such little people at so slight a cost! Just what does God require of me if I am to have these benefits? Not very much, and yet a great deal. This is a paradox, I know. But it is just the way Jesus put it. You have to lose yourself to save yourself; you have to give in order to have. The people I know to have the most are those who are the largest givers. Jesus Himself gave His life, and yet no one in all the world was ever richer than He.

Some good friends of mine invested their all in a soy bean factory. But after two floods they were completely wiped out. Every dime of savings, even their boy's college fund, was swept from out their hands. But did they give up and turn to curse God and grow bitter? No, they started all over again. On their nineteenth wedding anniversary they went out together to a hamburger shop for their anniversary dinner. It was all they could afford. As they sat there happy with each other they said, "Well, tonight we start exactly where we began when we were married nineteen years ago—with empty hands. But, come to think of it," they added, "we do have something. We have each other. We have our fine, clean-cut boy, and, best of all, we have faith that God will lead us safely on."

The next Sunday, as they had always done, they went to church. For church to them was not merely a refuge in time of trouble, but the place where they could meet God in prayer and worship, and renew their spiritual strength.

Some friends heard of the severe financial losses of the couple and wrote: "We've heard of what has happened to you. We want you still to believe what we were taught back there in Sunday school, that 'all things work together for good to them that love God.' We know that your Bill has set his heart on college. Well, God has blessed us abundantly. We know that you don't have the money now to send him. So enclosed is a receipt for his first year's tuition paid in full at Dubuque University." Who now will challenge my claim that if only we have faith in God things will work out to our good?

Give your life to God and God will give Himself to you. You will receive so very, very much for so very, very little!

CHAPTER XII

IT ISN'T EASY

IT IS NOT easy to be a Christian. It takes vastly more than everything a man has in him to be a Christian. Yet it is the most glorious life possible. Some would over-simplify and say, "Well, to be a Christian is simply to believe in the Lord Jesus Christ, and you are saved." True Holy Scripture makes clear that this is the narrow gate of faith. But Dwight L. Moody's remark to a man whose religion was patently shallow is most revealing. The man said, "I attended one of your meetings a year ago and I was saved."

"Well," said Dr. Moody, "the thing that interests me is what has happened since. What progress have you made in your Christian life?"

No one ever saunters into the kingdom with his hands in his pockets. People sometimes come to me very per-turbed, saying, "I have some stubborn doubts about the faith. I am discouraged about Christians in general and myself in particular. Can God possibly forgive me my doubts and falterings?" In my opinion honest doubts are actually the footprints of the Holy Spirit, and indicate a certain awareness. The mind is coming to grips with faith's mighty challenge to our easy-going paganism. Honest doubters who really pursue truth are the recipients of God's great promise: "If with all your heart ye truly seek me, ye shall surely ever find me. Thus saith the Lord." I believe Jesus deliberately chose St. Thomas as one of the twelve to represent the honest doubter. For in the great moment when he knelt before His risen Lord and exclaimed, "My Lord and my God!" Thomas pointed up the ultimate glorious goal of honest doubt.

Many mature Christians have moments when they wonder whether God will keep His every promise. Abraham did, and yet he is the only human being Scripture describes as "friend of God." Have you known a time of great disappointment when you were ready to throw up the sponge? You had prayed and yet God answered, "No," to your petition. Didn't Jesus have the same answer in Gethsemane's garden?

Considering today's topsy-turvey world, maybe you too have wondered how God's will actually ever will be done in our midst as it is done in Heaven. Will the kingdoms of this world ever become the Kingdom of our God and His Christ? St. Paul must have pondered the same question when he began his missionary journeys. For him, too, the Kingdom dragged on leaden feet, and at every turn he was rebuffed and thrust aside. But in the light of history look at the actual influence he had on a pagan world.

Jesus calls us to discipleship in the face of unnumbered difficulties. I like to think of Jesus' little band of disciples as a symphony orchestra. Some had major parts to play, others very minor parts. Some had loud instruments, like a bass drum or the bull 'cello, while others gave out only soft music, as from a piccolo or a flute. Yet every part was important to the beauty of the whole. Just so God has given each of us part in life's orchestra.

Some of us will get our names into headlines. Others will be completely passed by. But be sure of this, every loving deed and every unselfish investment will be written in the Book of Life. Is that not what really counts?

Oh, I am not so foolish as to try to win you to discipleship by telling you it is a sure way to success and that ever after you will be happy, well and prosperous. There will be crosses in every Christian's way. Some spiney thorns will stab deeply. We do not fight flesh and blood, but principalities and powers, and we must go through much tribulation to make our way to Heaven. We follow a leader who gasped out His last breath on a cross. It is not easy to be a Christian.

In God's great plan for our development, struggle and spirited battle play their necessary parts. When he was asked what his favorite Bible verse was an old minister, rich in experience said: "And it came to pass."

"Why, that is not even a verse," objected his interrogator.

"Oh, yes," insisted the parson, "that is my favorite verse. I think of it every time that trouble comes. It doesn't come to stay. It comes to pass!"

Anyone who has fought through obstacles to victory will agree that he and God are always a majority and more than a match for any foe.

Not long ago I stood with a missionary pastor looking up at Mount Mahru in Africa. This mountain stands all by itself. It is shaped like a pyramid, and there are no foothills. "One day I started early in the morning," said the pastor, "and I climbed to its summit and back again

by sunset." He made the achievement seem so easy that
I was almost afraid he would have me up before dawn to
go with him for his second try. "Why did you do it?" I
asked. "What possible incentive is there in climbing a
mountain?"

"Oh," he said, "the best answer to that are the words
of Mallory, conqueror of Everest, in answer to a similar
question, 'I climbed it because the mountain was there.'"

Man is always challenged by what is beyond his reach.
Something dies when life has no more mountains to scale.
The pastor's next remark serves my point even better. For
as we stood there he said, "No mountain is ever higher
than it is at the bottom." Think of what it would mean
if people instead of giving up when they face a problem
would decide, This is the worst than can happen. Then
after seeking God's grace, if they would start climbing,
the summit would soon beckon. No mountain is ever
higher than it is at its base.

Besides battles to fight, there are discouragements to
face. It is not easy to be a Christian. False witnesses helped
make Calvary for Jesus. His followers too, must often face
slander. I make plenty of mistakes in my ministry, but I
never expected to live in a charmed circle free from crit-
icism. Yet I must admit, humanly speaking, that anonymous letters with utterly false charges send my spirits
into a tailspin. I know something about Elijah's mood
when he cried, "It is enough. Take away my spirit." Is
there anything more impossible than trying to run false
slander to the ground? My experience is shared by many.
How do you feel when you see a man who uses his church
membership only as a front for unethical business prac-
tices? Jesus described such persons perfectly: "Wolves in

sheep's clothing." Some are so heartless as to steal the last penny of a widow. When I really get angry I feel that there ought to be some sifting followed by wholesale expulsion of hypocrites from church, but then I remember Jesus' parable of the tares growing up with the wheat. Moreover, I know that a church is a hospital for sick souls, and that all of us are sinners and therefore need the healing of the Gospel. So when it comes to winning this battle with the devil, the effective sermon of consistent Christian living in the home and at the store or office or on the street can go deeper than any sermon from this pulpit. Let no one expect to saunter into the Kingdom with his hands in his pocket.

One day the well-known Dr. S. Park stood in a busy railroad station. A ragged tramp sauntered along, and, as if accidentally, dropped a nickel beside him. The kind doctor bent down and retrieved the nickel and handed it back to the tramp. The tramp refused it, saying, "I dropped a fifty-cent piece, sir." Dr. Park insisted the coin was the same one that was dropped, but the tramp only became abusive. A crowd gathered, and, human nature being what it is, the crowd's sympathies were not at all with the well-dressed gentleman. The onlookers actually thought that he was holding out on the ragged, unkempt vagrant. When the police arrived, the floater was gone. When they questioned Dr. Park, he said, "Think of it! I had to give this man a dollar before I could be rid of him and extricate myself from the crowd. And all I wanted to do was to act like a Christian and help retrieve his nickel." Rebuffed in our attempts at well-doing we often wonder, "Does it pay to be a Christian?" But in the light of Christ we know that just there we first begin to prove our Christianity.

Afflictions and trials are the test that show the genuine from the spurious and demonstrate that we may feel assured that "to them that love God all things work together for good."

On a recent world tour, my companion and I planned a three-day rest in our strenuous itinerary. After the bitter cold of Europe's unprecedented winter, it seemed wonderful to relax on the white sands of the Indian Ocean at Durban, South Africa. I gave no thought to sunburn, deeming my leftover tan from summer camping protection enough. But when I was in the shower at the end of the day I looked at myself in the mirror and was horrified by the lobster-red hue of my body. No sleep was to be had that night. I thought seriously of going to the hospital. By morning even the touch of my sock sent me writhing. I was so roasted that I seemed ready to crack all over. I spent the rest of my time there in the shade on the wide veranda watching the rest enjoying themselves while I was peeling like an onion. That day the blue-bottle fish came in from deep sea and infested the shore waters. These surface fish have long stingers that are impregnated with poison. A thousand bathers had to have emergency aid, a hundred and fifty of them had to be hospitalized. Two narrowly escaped drowning only by the alertness of the lifeguards, since the poison paralyzes chest muscles. My companion's thoughtful comment will be remembered, "Misfortune can be good fortune."

"Must I be carried to the skies on flowery beds of ease?" asks a much loved hymn. The answer of course is no, for there are battles and disappointments, and our Leader came at last to a cross. A little lad followed his father on a rugged climb. At a particularly difficult turn the father called back, "Be careful, son!" Answered the boy, "Don't worry dad. I am putting my feet in your footprints."

You and I can safely follow the print of Jesus' feet as we make our way out into our community. Despite these black and cloudy days, there is hope in following Christ. In His Gospel is healing for the sickness of our world.

A passenger wearing a clerical collar on a trans-world plane was asked by a fellow passenger sitting next to him where he was going. "I am returning to France to bid my old mother good-by for the last time," answered the clergyman.

"What do you mean, the last time?" asked his chance acquaintance. "How can you be so certain that you will not see her again?"

Said the other, "I am a missionary to the Belgian Congo. The average white man's life span there is only two-and-one-half years."

His amazed questioner asked, "Why on earth, then, do you go back?"

The missionary was momentarily silent. One could almost see him visualizing the outstretched hands in that malarial dark corner of the world, without God and without hope. "Why will you go?" insisted his questioner.

The missionary said simply, "There is a man on the cross."

It isn't easy to be a Christian and know such a compulsion. But it is the most wonderful way of life this world has ever known!

CHAPTER XIII

LIVING VICTORIOUSLY

Then PILATE TOOK Jesus and scourged him." Scourging was a savagely cruel form of punishment of criminals. It was inflicted with a long rawhide lash studded with bits of lead. The jailers would bind the prisoner and lash his bare back until blood spurted from the broken skin. "And then Pilate took Jesus and scourged him."

Let me remind you that Jesus was both the Son of God and the son of man. As a human being He suffered pain as we suffer pain, the only difference being that He had in His divine nature the capacity to suffer infinitely. Then also remember that legions of Heaven's angels stood ready to defend Him at His slightest beck. "Then Pilate took Jesus and scourged him."

"God so loved the world that he gave his only Son" so that a bridge might be built from your hearts to eternity. That is why Jesus endured the mockery that ended His mock trial. First, they draped on Him a cast-off faded cloak of royal purple. Then they handed Him a reed as a mock scepter. For a crown they plaited together some thorny branches, which they pressed down on His head until the blood streamed down His cheeks. Then they made game of Him and jeered Him, shouting, "Hail, King of the Jews!" Did they mock Jesus because He had answered Pilate's question, "Art thou a king, then?" by saying simply, "Thou sayest it"? Now he stands uncringingly before Pilate, who says to his prisoner, "Don't you know that I have the power to release you or to deliver you to the cross?"

Jesus answered Pilate simply, "You have no power over me except the power given you from above." Let those key words stick in your mind like a burr in a sheep's fleece, for without God's power victory will never be ours!

Actually, Jesus was not on trial before Pilate. Pilate was on trial before Jesus. The proud Roman had his chance. I think that his sense of Roman justice bade him let Jesus go. I believe he was intelligent enough as a judge to know that Jesus was innocent, as indeed his words and actions attested. But Pilate was a coward. When the Jewish leaders clamored for Jesus' life Pilate remembered that there were a million Jews in Jerusalem as against his own limited garrison. But Pilate as a symbol is ageless. Every time we lack courage to stand up for our faith, Jesus is on trial before us. When we surrender to doubt and fear as did Pilate of old, we resentence Jesus to crucifixion.

Victory for us, too, will be hard won, the price costly. So let us consider what is demanded. First, a battle is involved. Pilate failed miserably in his crucial battle by giving in to his baser self. He acted entirely from selfish impulses and expediency. He forgot that history would coldly appraise his act and that we would not be able to escape the white light of eternity's judgment throne. Scripture warns us to "put on the whole armor of God" when we prepare for battle. And again, "Be strong in the Lord and in the power of his might." In our day it seems that these injunctions fall on deaf ears. Instead, we boast about our ingenuity and our brawn. Yet these have miserably failed us, as is witnessed by the fear abroad everywhere.

"Be strong in the Lord." Have we accepted the strength God offers us? Or do we depend on the gigantic Franken-stein monster, the robot with wheels within wheels for a brain and possessing frightening atomic powers, that we have constructed?

Go back with me to childhood days. Think of how fantastic some of our most commonly used modern inven-tions would have seemed to us as children had they been suddenly conjured up. Yet these things have been de-veloped in our own lifetime. Science has given man the fingers of radar with which to penetrate the densest fog. There have been occasions on my world travels when I couldn't imagine how a plane with visibility at zero could be safely set down on a narrow strip of concrete. Yet, by the miracle of radar, we made a safe landing. Science has given man the means to follow a football game while ensconced in the comfort of his own living room. It makes no difference that the rival elevens are playing three thousand miles away. Electronics can amplify the faintest whisper into a mighty shout that can be boosted around the whole world in the space of a second or two. Through the wonders of aeronautics man has developed wings so that now the remotest place in the world is only a few hours from one's nearest airport. In fact, man now can travel faster than sound.

What a fantastic world! And still we live with cold fear clutching at our hearts, all because of these almost im-measurable energies that we have conjured up. After the first H-bomb had been tested, it was clear that a single bomb dropped at the center of our nation's capital would wipe the beautiful city off the map.

On invitation from the secretary, I have appeared before the Senate Foreign Relations Committee in Washington. So now I know first-hand the fears that grip the hearts of our leaders. They earnestly seek an answer to the world problems, and, thank God, they are humble enough even to turn to Church and ask what program it can offer for our world's salvation. We are coming to see that God's plan for world peace, plainly given in His Word, can work only if enough individual Christians will have the daring to put it in action. It is in the light of this that I want you to know how really significant you are in your community as members of this congregation. Your Christian response as an individual could well start a chain reaction that would bring peace, so far as the world situation is concerned. Washington is jittery only because it realizes that our modern technology has created a soulless monster!

Yet these tremendous atomic energies and technological developments can be constructively used for good. But let a godless pagan hold the trigger, and the human race can easily be obliterated.

We are all in a state of jitters. Is it not because man has depended solely on himself rather than on God? I am no prophet, and still I am sure that unless God's power from above gets inside of us here below, then the forces of evil will destroy us. It is war to the finish!

We have our internal struggle too. So many people are tempted to give up and say, "What's the use?"

Eugene Field was a columnist. One day, feeling completely frustrated, he sent a note to his editor which read, "There'll be no column tomorrow. I am giving up."

106

You have felt that way, too, I am sure, and have thought, "What's the use? There is so much orneryness and sin abroad that it doesn't pay to be a Christian. Who cares and what's to the good?"

By return messenger the editor sent Field this note: "I have a fellow working on the linotype down in the basement. He has three children desperately ill with scarlet fever. He's not giving up." Thoroughly ashamed of his action, Eugene Field went to work and pounded out his best column.

Terrible days may well be ahead of us. And yet the challenge of them could lift us to a new height of great living. This will be true if we fight our battles with God-given weapons. These weapons are not A-bombs or H-bombs, which are mere human tools! The challenge of our day is to be as big in soul as we are big in ingenuity. This is possible if we use the sword of the Spirit of God by which only can we cut through the vast problems that confront our lives and our world.

"Remain constant in prayer," says Scripture. "Put on the whole armor of God . . ." Steep yourself in things spiritual and then translate your faith into daily living. Great things will begin to happen. Our gravest difficulty is that we have tried to live apart from God.

I thought it significant that United States Senators were interested in what the church was doing and what it could offer in this present world situation. Most thinking people will agree that the Point Four Program offers a constructive solution to the distress abroad. It emphasizes helping people help themselves. It proposes to translate the Good Samaritan teaching into action on a global scale in our twentieth century. It seeks to avoid pauperizing people by outright gifts. It would rather share with them the "know how" in developing their own countries. We are honestly trying to be unselfishly helpful.

Yet it is no secret that practically every country in the world is suspicious of us and wonders if we really come in good will. They suspect our offers of help are really deals for military bases, and that we seek to build up a number of dependent economic colonies. Senators with whom I talked are agreed that the Church has an unparalleled opportunity to expand its missionary activities further, and to continue aid in soil conservation and animal husbandry and in building more hospitals and schools. People in the vast underprivileged areas across the sea know by the work the Church already has done that we are not interested in aggression but are spurred on solely by love. If we come as representatives of Christian America, then this token program of sharing will be understood. It can be carried out successfully only by a dedicated task force whose members will live close to God and work out from that high level. So you as a member of this congregation are a very important person in the world today.

As pastor of this church I am thrilled to find so many high-school and college students and young couples interested in things spiritual. It stirs my heart just to think of the spiritual potential they represent. My growing conviction is that a wholesale dedication of lives here would be tremendously felt even to the corners of the world. It is not out of pride in our accomplishments that I say this, but as a simple witness to the power of Almighty God working through individuals to change the community. Change the community first, and then can we hope to change the world. Join now the army of the Lord.

CHAPTER XIV

THE CURE FOR TROUBLED HEARTS

As a PREACHER, my most difficult task is to picture God adequately. How can the finite mind fully grasp the infinite? Can you teach Hebrew to an infant or logarithms to a toddler? Yet I have always felt I am nearer succeeding on Mother's Day than at any other time. If you will think of a Christian mother's self-sacrificing spirit, her concern for her children's welfare, her willingness to die rather than that harm come to her children, you have grasped in small measure what God is like.

Naturally, as I speak about God today a mother's dear face will come to many a mind. The little children singing at our services will appreciate this artless story. A little boy was just beginning to walk. You know how clumsy little boys are when they take their first steps. They stumble and fall even on a wrinkle of the carpet. So mother thought to make it easier for her little boy. She tied her apron string around the boy's waist, saying, "Now, if you fall just pull yourself to your feet again by this apron string." The boy readily caught on. When he stumbled he just held on to that apron string and was helped up again. He grew normally until at last he was tall enough to look out the window. He saw green grass, yellow flowers, and the majestic purple mountains in the distance. One day he said, "Mother, won't you untie this apron string so that I can go down the road and see all this beauty better?" Wise mother said, "No, my son, you are hardly strong enough yet. You need mother's help a little while still." However, one day when the door was ajar the boy saw his chance. Tugging hard, he loosed the string and slipped out the door, the apron string fluttering behind in the wind. He thought to himself, "Mother's apron string wasn't so strong after all."

As he trudged along he reveled in the grass and flowers. But it got late. A heavy mist arose from the swampy lowlands. At last he could not see where he was going and suddenly tumbled over a precipice. But the apron string caught on a bush. There he hung suspended by the apron string and swinging over the chasm like a pendulum. Tugging hard on the string he was able to pull himself to safety. As he started home he said, "I never thought mother's apron string could be so stout." Thinking back to the hot-blooded years of youth, who here does not remember saying over and over again, "Why do I always have to keep doing what mother and father ask? They are old-fashioned, anyway. Don't they know I am growing up?" But now grown older and wiser, we know our parents' way was for the best, and our love and esteem has bound them to us to the end of memory. So can it also be with God's commands and our love for Him.

God's faithfulness is like a mother's. He will follow us to the ends of the earth. Rudyard Kipling put it well when he wrote: "If I were hanged on the highest hill, I know whose love would follow me still, mother o'mine, O mother o'mine!"

Of Jesus it is written, "Having loved his own, he loved them to the end." Whatever dangers we may face, God will steadfastly stand with us. And so when we think about troubled hearts and how that God's love is like that of a mother's, I desire earnestly to bring to your minds three of the great troubles that cause us to fail, especially since they may affect every one of us.

The first is doubt. Are you tormented by doubts? Here is Jesus' antidote: "Believe in God," He says. "Believe also in me." It is for a Christian to know doubt. Bailey aptly says, "Who never doubted never half believed." Who hasn't asked himself, "Are these wonderful promises of God really true?" The disciples were doubt-ridden when Jesus said, "Behold, I go up to Jerusalem to suffer and die on a cross." They stubbornly remonstrated, saying, "Lord, that must never happen to you." And when it came to pass, they were bewildered and questioning. Thomas persisted in his doubt even after the other ten had told him that Jesus had appeared to them. And who of us hasn't been riddled by doubts at one time or another? In fact, sometimes I believe Jesus deliberately chose Thomas to represent us who are so slow to believe. One thing this old world of ours needs more than anything else is a personal faith in God born of deep conviction. I mean personal as apart from an abstract, intellectual faith about God. That can be a head-knowledge only, whereas I am speaking of a heart-accepted belief. Jesus' words in the Gospel of John are significant: "Believe in God." He didn't say, "Believe about God."

In journeying about the world I have talked to a number of refugee children who had to be evacuated from their homes. One such little girl who probably had lost all contact with her parents I found huddled in a corner, weeping. Others dutifully had prepared for bed, but she stood there disconsolately sobbing. Perhaps she was saying to herself, "What was it mother told me to do if ever I became lonely?" Perhaps she imagined what her mother would have done if she had been at her side in this faraway land, and so have been comforted. But how vastly different if mother had walked into the room to sit down on her bed, and say, "Here I am, darling, what can I do to help you?" What a vast difference between believing about somebody or believing in somebody. A significant phrase in our creed that we skip over far too lightly is: "I believe in God the Father Almighty, Maker of heaven and earth." You see, we believe in a personal God whom we can trust. I am positive that if it weren't for your faith many of you would have been missing from your pew here today.

Maybe it is despair that troubles you. To despair does not mean that you have lost your faith, or that you have given up God. There come times in counseling with people when I hardly know where to turn. Some lives take on a crazy pattern. Many have said something like this: "Every morning is just like every other morning. I go to work or I stay home to do my housework. I draw my pay check and pay my bills and then go to bed again at night. Life has become one monotonous daily routine." The enamel of living is badly chipped for them. Anything like song and hope has died out. They ask, "How can one recover the joy of living?" And so they are jumpy and irritable and appear ready to fly to pieces at any moment. They are forever living with the frayed ends of their nerves showing.

"Is there any cure for that kind of trouble?" they ask

despairingly. Out of this tragic emptiness is heard the whining, "What is the use of living?" I tell them, "If you will but take God at His word there is everything in the world to live for." If you will take these steps: Go regularly to church. Do you let the most trivial excuses cheat you of the communion with God? Are you one of those who each Sunday must hold a debate whether or not to go? How devastating and soul destroying! Jesus, "as his custom was," found Himself regularly in the synagogue. Commune regularly at the Lord's table! Irregular food habits are not conducive to health. Do you regularly seek out His table for spiritual nourishment of soul? Take time to read God's Word daily. This is a *must* ingredient of the prescription for a troubled heart. Along with these, take time each day to visit with God in prayer. Surely you follow your doctor's orders when you are ill. You do if you believe in your doctor. Here is one of the Great Physician's instructions: "They that wait upon the Lord shall mount up as eagles. They shall run and not be weary. They shall walk and faint not." Here is another: "For I am persuaded that neither life nor death, nor angels nor principalities nor powers, nor things present, nor things to come, nor height, nor depth, nor any other creature shall be able to separate us from the love of God, which is in Christ Jesus, our Lord." With such tremendous power available for the asking, need anyone despair?

These are not empty words. The great Apostle Paul proves that. What staying power he knew who could list this record: "Five times I have received at the hands of the Jews the forty lashes less one. Three times I was beaten with rods; once I was stoned; three times I have been shipwrecked, etc." Moreover, he knew a nagging, depressing

113

pain which he referred to as a "thorn in the flesh." Yet his faith never faltered. The secret of his power he willingly shared: "For to me to live is Christ." He invites everyone to walk with him at the side of the Saviour, that we too may be "more than conquerors through him that loved us."

Many of the upstanding men of this congregation are experts in the field of investments. It seems foolish to remind them that it pays to invest one's life in the things that will last forever. In the mad scramble of our reeling world why are many still tempted to trade their eternal inheritance for a mess of pottage? I have seen men who were self-sufficient and proud when things went well become like little children who were hurt and lost from mother's arms when caught in life's cruel upsets. Life can quickly become much like what happened to a little boy I saw building castles in the sand by the sea. He is so absorbed in his play. Now he stands back proudly viewing his work. It never occurs to him that the tide is coming in and that one wave will wash everything away. It is even so when the cold wave of death sweeps down upon us. A moment and everything, our stocks and our bonds and all our proud accomplishments, are gone. But coming back again to our boy by the sea, the water has now backed him up against the cliff. Already the tide is up to his knees. He is shrieking and cringing in fear, even as many do before death's swift wave. But, lo, his elder brother stands on the ledge above. He is reaching down his strong arms to lift brother to safety. With good reason, Jesus is called our elder brother. His power and His strength are more than sufficient to lift us to a safe place. Faith in Him is simply your hands clasping His mighty outstretched, saving arm.

A little five-year-old boy had done wrong. Said his mother, "Son, you have made a mistake; we will have to do something about it." Then she threw her arms around him and kissing him, saying, "But I want you to know that I love you just the same." In my Bible I read about another boy, years older, who went into sin's far-away country and steeped himself in sodden living. Sick and forsaken, he comes to himself and decides at long last to make his way home to his father. The father got word of his coming and went a long way on the road to meet him. He threw his arms around his son as he said, "Son, you made a mistake; we will have to do something about it. But I love you just the same." God is just like that, says Jesus.

Again I ask, What is your trouble? Is it doubt? "Believe in God," says Jesus. "Believe also in me." What is your trouble? Is it despair? Jesus says, "I am the way, the truth and the life." Why not try going God's way? What is your trouble? Is it fear of death? Listen to Jesus: "In my Father's house are many mansions. I go to prepare a place for you, . . . that where I am, there ye may be also." What more wonderful promise could there be than that? So "let not your heart be troubled."

CHAPTER XV

HAVE YOU MADE YOUR CHOICE?

LIKE A BOAT that has drifted to the edge of Niagara, life too, has its point of no return. We may be postponing our decision to follow after Jesus. We may reason that so much of life's pleasure is still untasted and that Jesus places galling restrictions and inhibitions on us. But mark this well, my friends, God's Word warns us sharply against the point of no return. So long as we are still open to persuasion and are willing to seek guidance of God, we may be certain that we have not reached that dangerous point. But if we delay too long then our ears will grow deaf to His still, small voice, until, at last, we will have lost control over choice itself. We will have reached the point of no return.

Are you prepared to make your choice? Such readiness involves two steps. First of all, you will have to discard your cloak of self-righteousness, which means that you must forever quit relying on your own effort. You must throw yourself entirely on God's mercy.

You may think that with so many children to care for God cannot bother about your little life, so you let your problems get you down. One of the reasons that Jesus came into our world was to identify Himself with the ordinary problems of the common man. He was tempted as we are. He felt our joys and sorrows. Didn't He weep at Lazarus' grave and mingle His tears with the tears of Lazarus' sisters? He knows our need.

I often think of the little boy I saw sitting outside of the walls of Versailles. He was holding a little sparrow with a broken wing. A kindly lady came along and she asked, "Sonny, would you like me to take this sparrow home and nurse it back to health? I promise I will bring it back to these gardens when it is healed and let it fly free again."

The little boy thought for a moment. Then he said, "If you don't mind, Madam, I will take care of the bird myself." He paused momentarily and added, "Because, you see, I understand this poor bird."

The woman could not quite get what that boy meant until he stood up. Then she saw his left leg was in a cast. Because he was crippled, he understood the suffering bird's problem.

The God whom I know became incarnate in Jesus Christ and came into the world to learn what problems I must face in life so that He can match the strength I may need in order to face those problems triumphantly. That is why, when I walk with Him, I can have such confidence.

If you are ready for anything, not only do you discard your cloak of self-righteousness, but you accept the righteousness of God as a free gift. You put on His cloak of perfect righteousness.

A man was having great trouble and was sorely confused. In counseling with his minister, he was advised: "Go home and write in one column all the wrongs you

117

have done, and in a second enumerate all the good that you have done."

When he reported, the man said that he had written and written and still had not come to the end of the list of all the wrongs he had done. The only good thing with which he could credit himself was that he had loved his mother. "Finally," he said, "I erased that because I did not think I had loved her enough."

The minister asked, "Then what did you do, my friend?"

The man answered, "After I had looked at all those wrongs I had done, I dropped to my knees and I just thanked God that in Christ I had a Saviour from all sin. I knew that I just could never hope to even up that score by myself." He was a wise man to accept God's forgiveness and claim His righteousness.

There is one sense in which we are the masters of our fate. Each of us will determine for himself whether he will accept God's help and guidance or risk his soul on the brink of destruction. Either we accept God or we reject Him.

Do you realize the importance of the choices you make? Why your eternal destiny hinges on what you choose? Do you realize what are the joys God means for you to enjoy here and now? Do you realize that by His power you can conquer any obstacle in this world, that you can rise up out of the ashes of defeat into glorious victory? You can lose everything materially and still draw on the exhaustless treasure of Heaven. All this is yours for the asking. God means that you may have it.

This does not mean that you can persist in sinning and still expect God to take you back again whenever you wish. A father told his boy this story of a good shep-

118

herd: "A sheep crawled through a hole in the fence to wander off into a far country. When the shepherd missed his sheep, he went out to seek it. Fortunately the shepherd was in the nick of time to rescue it from ravenous beasts. Rejoicing, he carried it home to the safety of the fold again." When the father finished his dramatic story, the boy turned to him and asked, "Then did he patch up the hole in the fence so that the sheep could not get out another time?"

That was a good question. There is much more to the Christian life than simply a passive acceptance of God's forgiveness. It is to allow God to patch up the holes in our lives so that we do not break out again at the same place to get all tangled in sin another time. We cannot live in sin and apart from God without paying the price of suffering. I am not speaking now of physical suffering. Physical pain cannot compare with the torment of an outraged conscience. This is the worst torment that can be experienced.

I am encouraged that people are turning to God these days. Openly they talk about their faith. Business men are unashamedly talking about it to their office associates. They are recognizing their human limitations, both physical and spiritual. When they become nervous and tense, they have learned to pause for a little talk with God. Many tell me that immediately a great calm has come into their soul and that they have been helped to meet their problems with sure confidence. I know exactly what they are talking about, because it so perfectly parallels what has been my personal experience.

Dan Towler plays for the Los Angeles Rams, a professional football team. He was voted the outstanding professional player in the all-star pro game in January, 1952. Before the important game he went to his coach, and suggested, "I don't know what you think about this, but I would like to suggest that before every game our squad observe a few moments of silence so that each one of us can pray to God in his own words."

The coach was a little surprised at the suggestion, but he said he would arrange it. Dan Towler told his team-mates, "Fellows, I don't believe that God will miraculously help us win football games, but I think if we come to peace within ourselves, if we are unified personalities, we will play better football."

This is what Dan Towler reported: "We prayed with all our might and then we went out on the field and played with all our might."

Do you see that combination—to pray to God as if everything depended solely on Him and then to go into life and live it to the fullest as if everything depended on you? That is partnership in its finest sense. Use the resources God has given you. Pray to Him for wisdom to put these resources to the best possible advantage!

A fifty-four-year-old man died unexpectedly. One friend remarked to another, "It is too bad, isn't it, that he didn't have a chance to prepare?"

"What do you mean?" asked the other. "He had fifty-four years to prepare!"

How old are you? You have had that many days, then, to get ready. Is your craft headed toward shore and away from the rapids or is it drifting past redemption point down toward the rapids just beyond the bend? Have you made your choice?

CHAPTER XVI

ACCEPT THE KING'S INVITATION

IN HER BOOK, *Uncle Tom's Cabin,* Harriet Beecher
Stowe has one of her characters quote the much-loved
verse, "Come unto me, all ye that labor and are heavy
laden, and I will give you rest." Old black Tom listens
to this word with face aglow. Then he turns to say to the
speaker, "Them's great words. But who says them?" That,
of course, is the important thing. Anyone can make promises, but if the promises have nothing behind them they
mean nothing. A woman went to a lawyer to draw up her
will. She bequeathed vast sums to churches and to favorite charitable institutions. Finally, the lawyer became
a little suspicious. He turned to the woman and said:
"Where do you have your money?"

The lady said, "I really don't have any. I am just making
out this will to show my good intentions."

If I were to stand in my pulpit mouthing promises
with no resources back of them my words would be mean-
ingless. How grateful I am to be the representative of
Jesus Christ and to bring His followers the great promises
of Him who is Lord of lords and King of kings.

Many invitations to high places have come to me, an
humble minister of the Gospel. To have such opportuni-

ties to sit down with the great personalities of Church and State throughout the world has much enriched my life. Yet it comes to me in retrospect that another invitation far more significant has come to all of us, whether we be of high estate or low, rich or poor, educated or uneducated, whether we have traveled around the world or never put step beyond our own little community. It is the greatest invitation anybody could possibly receive, and I hold it up before you. Addressed to you as children of the heavenly Father, it reads, "Come unto me, all ye that labor and are heavy laden, and I will give you rest." Surely these words rank among the greatest of Holy Writ.

One needs only read them to feel the cheer and power they infuse into one's life. The King of kings is speaking, "Take my yoke upon you and learn of me, for my burden is light, and ye shall find rest to your souls." Lives there a man with a soul so dead that he does not yearn for this peace and rest from the sore labors of living?

An elderly minister was overcome with emotion while preaching on this text. Though he had read and reread these beautiful phrases countless times his voice choked with deep feeling. He said to his people: "What does it mean, 'Come unto me'—what does it mean?" A little girl raised her hand and said, "Pastor, I know what it means. It means that Jesus wants me." What a Bible commentary. We could dip into the most learned commentaries in vain to get a better light on this word. "It means Jesus wants me." Friends, repeat that to your heart. That is what Jesus, God's Son, really is saying.

Now, who are the weary in this world? I thought of the disciples as I mulled over this text. I said to myself, "Maybe doubting Thomas typifies the weariest, most guilt-

122

laden person that ever walked this world." How his doubts must have eaten like an acid, burning deep into his mind. He wanted to believe, but unbelief crept over him like a London pea-soup fog, filling heart and soul. There are folks in our day who seek an anchorage for their faith. Yet they are too proud and sophisticated to accept salvation at Jesus' hand. For you must believe in order to have it. Are not they asking for a little God who nearly fits into the measure of their mind? People want to reason things out for themselves.

Then I thought again that perhaps it is John who better represents the weariest person. John was an idealist. He looked for the Kingdom of God to come in an outward manner. But when John observed how people acted, the conflict between what should be and what was, it bewildered and confused him, even as many people are bewildered and confused today.

Again I thought, Peter is my man, the type of the most weary. Does he not typify the person who comes to church on Sunday? He wants to serve God, but his life is inconsistent. His deeds do not fit his profession. You will remember that it was Peter who denied Jesus on the night He was betrayed, when His friends would have counted most. But as I reflected further, I rejected each of these in turn.

Then I stopped with Judas. He was the personification of selfishness. Did he not sell his Lord for thirty paltry pieces of silver? He used for his own ends the slender treasury entrusted to him by his fellow disciples. He sourly objected to their sharing any money with the poor. The last glimpse we have of him hurtling himself down on the rocks of Hinnom valley speaks of the intolerable burden he no longer could bear. Here, then, is my weariest person in the world. One like him would never give himself or his time, money, and talents to serve Christ in His church. He is looking out solely for number one.

How refreshing to meet the man who works for God. He makes his vocation, whatever it is, holy and separated unto the Lord. Such a man knows the peace of God in his heart. I have met countless such men and women. I make this my thesis: Peace comes only to individuals totally committed to God.

If you, then, accept the King's invitation you will know not only peace, but you also will know His mighty purpose for living. He says, "Take my yoke upon you." Look closely at this instruction. What possible attraction can a yoke have? Let us go back in our imagination to the day of Christ. A yoke was always for two. It distributed the burdens. It concentrated the pull of the load where the whole strength of the animal could be put to it. It was always for two. What is Jesus saying but, "Move over and I will add my strength to yours. I will step into the tugs and pull with you." My brief farm experience included watching a young colt broken to harness. I still remember the wild-eyed young thing, now shying sideways, then rearing and plunging at the touch of the unfamiliar harness being put on him. Look at him now, tossing his head, champing at the bit until the saliva looks like seafoam in his mouth. What are they doing? They are harnessing him with an old draft animal. The old plug does all the pulling at first. But at length his steadiness is contagious. The young frightened thing is now pulling his share at the side of the old draft horse like a veteran. This is something like what Jesus means.

Yokes were never laid on the back of an ox to give him exercise. He was harnessed for a purpose. The following glorious little legend has a beautiful lesson. When God created the birds He made them without wings. Then, with no word of explanation, God came along one day and placed wings on their backs. They murmured at first about the extra weight and the clumsiness they felt. Then one day one of them, being hotly pursued, ran with all possible speed. His wings fluttered in the wind. Suddenly he began to flap them in the wind. A strange exhilaration came over him. He discovered that he was being lifted up. Soon a wide gap of absolute safety was between him and his enemies. He was beyond reach of cruel fang or gory talon. How happy all the birds became after that lesson.

Without looking too hard, each of us can find a red thread of purpose in the shifting experiences that come our way. One day a little Sunday-school girl was told about the yokes. She asked, "Why did they put that clumsy, heavy thing on the poor animal's neck? Surely that would make sores and only add to his load."

The teacher explained as well as she could. It really made it easier for the ox to pull the plow. And then the teacher turned to the little girl, asking, "Now what do you think is meant by the yoke of God?" The little girl answered, "It must mean that God puts His arms around me." Once again, out of the mouths of babes and children God has ordained not only praise but understanding. The child's word has put the light of eternal worth on every life.

Acceptance of the King's invitation not only brings peace and purpose, but power for living as well. This is a jittery age. Men are confused and bewildered. E. Stanley

Jones talks about "Confusionist Christians." Every one of us knows what he means. Look at the man on the street. Observe people in their social relationships. All are trying to get something out of this world that can never be found —a deep, inner satisfaction that everyone must have for real living. It is this gnawing hunger in our hearts that drives us to our churches for worship. The words of Jesus, "Come unto me, all ye that labor and are heavy laden, and I will give you rest," answer our deepest need. If we sincerely desire to find that peace Jesus puts the key in the words, "Learn of me." Here is our clue.

Early in my ministry I determined that each year I would seek out an outstanding minister and live with him for a week. I would watch him at his work. I would go with him on pastoral calls. I would ask him to take me into his inner confidence. These many years now I have faithfully continued this practice. Some of the great men of God whom I have interviewed come to mind. I freely acknowledge that I am head over heels in debt for the inspiration, the wisdom, and the insights they have shared with me. There is really only one way to know a person. Live with him. And the only way that we can really know God is to be with Him not only during the brief hour of a Sunday morning service, but day by day.

Someone said facetiously that he had a "nodding" acquaintance with God. (Did he mean the sleepy hour he spent in a church service?) Yet if you come to live with God no stress can harm your soul. This week I read again the familiar story of how one day Jesus found His disciples by the sea mending their nets. He asked to be ferried across to the other side. They obeyed immediately. And as they were out in the midst of the Sea of Gennesaret,

Jesus fell asleep on a pile of nets up in the front. At about the blackest hour of midnight a sudden squall came up. The waves beat against that weathered little boat. But, despite the tossing of the boat and the howling wind, Jesus' slumber was undisturbed. The disciples, sailors though they were, became mortally afraid. They shook Jesus to awaken Him. With voices tense with fear they cried, "Master, get up quickly! We will all perish unless you help." Jesus awakened, and with one glance had everything in hand. He took His stand on the deck of the little craft, faced the angry waves, and lifted His hand. And in a voice heard above the frightful gale, He said, "Peace, be still!" At once there was a great calm. The angry waves became little ripples, and the wind was no more than a murmur.

I share with you a method that has never failed me in the pinches of my life. I promise that if you will try it, it will work for you, too. When temptation comes, summon up a mental image of Christ. Let it fill your mind. His lips will move and to you, too, He will say, "Peace, be still!" We but put to the test a promise that St. Paul tried. Listen to his word in his first letter to the Corinthians, the tenth chapter, the thirteenth verse:* "But God can be trusted not to allow you to suffer any temptations beyond your powers of endurance. He will see to it that every temptation has a way out, so that it will never be impossible for you to bear." Look this Jesus, your God and King, full in the face. Your fears must then fold their tents like the Arabs and as silently glide away. When next you are nervous or jittery, caught in one of life's sudden storms

* Quoted from *Letters to Young Churches,* by J. B. Phillips (Macmillan).

that threatens to tear your life apart, lift up your eyes and see those gentle hands raised in blessing. Is Jesus not saying to you, "Peace, be still"? Have you a problem too heavy to carry alone? Let Jesus, strong Son of God, put His shoulder beneath it. He truly is present. He keeps His promise, "Lo, I am with you always." The invitation comes to you personally today:

> Come to the Saviour, make no delay,
> Here in His word He has shown us the way—
> Here in our midst He is standing today
> Tenderly saying, "Come."

A doctor paused at my church door as I shook his hand following a recent service. He said, "I wish I had that kind of medicine to give people who come to me for help and healing." I was humbled to think that I had represented the Great Physician that day and given out of His power. Out of the crucible of unnumbered experiences I can assure you, "Earth has no sorrow that Heaven cannot heal!"

CHAPTER XVII

GOD'S ATTORNEY

Y OUR HEART IS a courtroom. Every day a trial takes place there. It is quite significant to recognize that the mere fact of becoming a Christian does not necessarily guarantee you will remain a Christian. There is always a possibility of falling from grace, for we are tempted daily. However, at the end of each day we can choose an attorney to represent us as we render our account.

There is one Attorney who is able to plead for us successfully and win the help that we need, but one only. "There was none other good enough to pay the price of sin; Christ only can unlock the door of Heaven and let us in." At the end of each day, just as at the end of life, this great Advocate is willing to take His stand beside us and plead our cause. He is willing to take upon Himself our guilt and our transgressions in order that His Father's verdict, rendered according to strictest justice, may be, "Not guilty." For, after all, it is a hard and fast rule of justice that a second penalty may not be exacted. The burden of our guilt and sin will then roll off our shoulders into Calvary's gaping hole, and our souls will know, instead, the peace and freedom that forgiveness accords.

We must decide who is to represent us. We must

choose Jesus as our Advocate. He will never force Himself upon us. Amid the babel of conflicting voices in our world today only the still, small voice of God can really bring us true peace. We cannot evade this responsibility of choosing. Pilate and Herod each tried vainly to shift responsibility. Pilate dramatically called for a basin of water and made a public spectacle of disclaiming his responsibility for the verdict against Jesus. But Pilate could never wash Jesus' blood from his hands. History puts the blame squarely at his door. "Each man decideth which way his soul shall go."

On reaching the age of sixty, a doctor faced up to the accounting that one day he would have to give for every act of his life. A great fear came upon him as he thought of his missteps and misdeeds. "If only the heavenly Father would grant me one request," he said to himself, "what would be the most wonderful thing I could ask of Him?" As the doctor pondered this, he decided it would be God's permission to go back and live his life all over again, with the rich background that experience had given him. Who hasn't wished there could be a land of beginning again?

"Like a flash of lightning," continued the doctor, "there came to my consciousness that this is exactly what God is doing. Every day is in reality a world born anew. I can start over again. When I confess my sins and make a clean breast of everything before God, I receive from this righteous Judge the verdict, 'Not guilty.' Then acting in a simple trust, I stand on the threshold of the land of beginning again. I can live today by taking advantage of the mistakes I made yesterday and gleaning lessons from them as I start over again." What a tremendous thought to keep in mind!

Then it should follow that we ask, "If Jesus will do all this for me, what is there for me to do?" We do have the Attorney's fees to pay. Let three words tell the whole of the cost in the coin of His realm.

First of all, ask. If we already possess something, we are not likely to ask for it. Feeling self-sufficient, we will hardly assume the beggar's role and ask for what we have. But, to the contrary, if we feel desperately in want, we will ask for what we need. It is to this point that God wants to bring us, because He will not force Himself on us. We are all as guilty as sin and so desperately in need of a Saviour. Nothing could be dearer to God's heart than to hear us ask His forgiveness and His direction and help in our living.

A man dreamed that he saw Jesus tied hand and foot to a whipping post. A soldier with a lead-studded whip was lashing the naked body of the Master. The dream was so real to the man that he writhed on his bed in horror as he saw Jesus' bare back livid with welts and the blood spurting and running down His side. He thought the ordeal would never end. The soldier himself exhausted, bent His arms back to give our Lord just one more lash. The dreamer could stand it no longer. He rushed up as if to grab the assaulting arm. But before he could take hold of him, the soldier turned around. The man looked full into this face and to his horror discovered it to be his very own.

If we but look closer at the Calvary scene, we will find ourselves there. It wasn't that time on Calvary only two thousand years ago that Jesus was crucified. Every time we push Him away in self-sufficiency, every time we transgress His will, we pound more nails through His yielding hands and feet to make a fresh Calvary. We take the whips in our hands and lash His body. Who can count his Calvaries? Let us, then, ask for forgiveness, we who stand in such desperate need of it.

The second thing Jesus asks for as fee for representing us before the bar of justice is that we seek. Seeking implies earnest asking plus action. There is something that we, too, must do. We are not just to sit idly by and expect God to drop things into our laps. God gives us a share in answering our prayers and solving our particular problems. He honors our personalities by pouring in them His powers in response to our asking. He enables us, but always to the measure of our desire. We may be on the right track, but that will not do us any good if we simply sit there. Dad Elliot once said, "Life is like railroad tracks, mighty good to travel on, but the poorest possible place to lie down on." Now you understand my call for action!

There can be nothing at all lackadaisical about the Christian life. First, we commit the Golden Rule to memory, then we must commit the Golden Rule to life. I like what that country parson told his congregation about the Gospel. He said, "First, you got to believe it, and then you got to behave it." That means putting the Gospel into action and into shoe leather.

All of us possess many capabilities. Many ways of laboring with the Lord are open to us. But I am sure not one of us is giving to God as much as he can of himself. A man once said, "Look at those hands of yours. Consider how many are the uses they have, just your hands alone. With them you can clasp a friend's hand in a warm greeting of friendship, or you can clench your fists and strike a cruel blow. If you were an artist, you could take a brush and paint a beautiful picture; or, if a surgeon, you could take a knife and skillfully perform an operation."

Just think what it would be like if the whole of our life were committed to God. There is so much to do in this world, and God offers us the privilege of being yokefellows with Him. By brushing aside this offer with a self-sufficient shrug we are choosing someone other than God to represent us. God wants His Kingdom to come and His will to be done on earth as it is in heaven.

We preachers make the tragic mistake of pointing out the sins of commission almost exclusively. We become past masters in highlighting the things people do that are wrong and miserably fail to point out the great areas of omission and the times without number that we sidestep our responsibilities to our age. Those neglected areas begin right at home in our community. "O unattempted loveliness. O costly valor never won!"

A facetious boy asked his arithmetic teacher one day, "Teacher, can a person be punished for something he hasn't done?"

The teacher replied, "No, of course not."

"Okay, then," said the lad gloatingly, "I haven't done my arithmetic lesson."

Well, we can be punished for something we have left undone, and still God's justice will not be violated. I fear that much of the bill of particulars against any of us will be made up of those things we have failed to do in Christ's behalf.

The third part of our payment is that we must knock. Now this means that we will persistently seek God's will, and, finding it, be willing to do something about it. The oft-repeated story of the little boy who fell out of bed one night illustrates my point. His mother asked him the next morning, "Son, how came you to fall out of bed?"

"Mother," he said, "I guess I fell asleep too close to where I got in."

In my opinion, people are forever falling asleep too close to where they climbed into the Christian Church. There is so much to do and so little time in which to do it! We need to be in dead earnest about our main business of winning the world for Christ's Kingdom.

A man engaged in conversation a Communist who had put a leaflet in his hand. He advised the Communist, "It is no use, you will never get any place doing this. At best there are but two hundred thousand Communists in America, while we Christians number seventy-five million."

The Communist replied, "Remember Gideon's band? They had only three hundred. Members of my party are willing to live on the barest necessities of life. Every dime we earn above and beyond our simple needs we turn back to our cause; for we believe in it with all our hearts." Then he went on to say, "We are going to be victorious, and, if you want to know, I will tell you why. We have an unshakable faith in our cause. We are even willing to die for it. That is more than you are willing to do!" Is it? How far will you go to serve *your* cause?

CHAPTER XVIII

THE KEY TO THE KINGDOM

GLORY, POWER, STRENGTH, hope, eternity—all of us want these. How can we find them? When darkness closes in, our spirits cry out, "Is there no light to lead me? Is there no way of escape out of this dilemma?"

There is a way of escape out of any darkness or corner in which we may find ourselves. There is no problem that can defeat us if we will but put our trust in God. All of us need to be assured of this day by day.

The Kingdom of God offers sanctuary for everyone. You say, in effect, "Tell me, preacher, what is the key to the Kingdom and what do you mean by the term you so frequently use in the pulpit, the Kingdom of God?" In answering, let me ask, "What is your conception of the Kingdom of God?" Many of you would say that it is some future state of bliss in eternity which we hope to attain to at journey's end. Our conception of Heaven, at first thought, is usually the Kingdom of God coming to its consummation and glory in "the sky by and by." That is one way to picture the Kingdom of God, and it is a true one. Nor need we apologize for thus picturing it. The Kingdom will come in perfection and glory in the life that is to be.

But there is much more than that to the Kingdom of God. There are people hard at work in our communities helping to alleviate human suffering and build up better relations among the races. Men and women of good will strive for peace. Many hands are helping to build God's Kingdom in the community where we live.

But the concepts of walking with God in white forevermore and the concept of a richer, fuller, and happier life here on earth still do not complete the meaning of the Kingdom of God. It has a third dimension, the Kingdom of God within us. An additive of power and strength that comes from living and walking with God takes over in the inner recesses of our souls and hearts. Christ takes His throne to reign within as King of kings and Lord of lords.

How do I get hold of this key to the Kingdom? Scripture answers simply, "Except one be born again, he cannot see the kingdom of God." We are destined to fumble blindly at a locked door whose key has been flung away unless we are willing in humility and penitence to go through the process of being born again. For this new life comes only through faith in Christ.

What is it to be born again? What must I do to get in my hand the key that unlocks the door to a new life and releases this strength within my soul? How I love the answer Jesus makes, for it belongs to us all. He doesn't single out a favored few. He has chosen every one of us to come to Him and be saved. Nor do we have to hold a doctorate in theological dogma to qualify. On my knees I thank God that this is not the answer. We do not have to possess a great intellect to hold the key to the Kingdom. To the contrary, Jesus says, "Except one become as a little child, he cannot inherit the kingdom of God." This is the kindest and most generous thing Jesus could possibly have said, because it opens the door for any of us who will choose His way.

Coming back to the key, Jesus has clearly stated, "Unless we become as little children we cannot enter the kingdom." What qualities of the child must I have to possess the key? In the first place we must be receptive even as children. So many of us are at war against ourselves. We will never admit that we are wrong; we will not admit that we need help. Oh, if only we would acknowledge our inadequacies, how much stronger we would be mentally and physically. If we would explore the Scriptures and learn of the saints' experience we would know how real God is and find our way to the Kingdom.

Some people ridicule the idea that God, with a universe to run, could possibly be concerned with the lot and fortune of man. Yet, not one of us can know pain or heartache which does not concern Almighty God. He demonstrated that beyond all shadow of doubt when Jesus walked here among men. I love what St. Mark records: "And Jesus stood still"—He had heard a blind beggar's cry above the noise of the crowd and stopped. He who was on God's errand to save the world stopped to let this beggar at the dusty roadside fill His ear with his sad story. When little children came to Him, He didn't chase them away. Instead, He reprimanded the disciples for pushing them aside. The disciples thought He ought to busy Himself with greater things and not stoop to talk with babies and doting women. They were wrong, "For of such is the kingdom of God," Jesus told them.

A friendly little girl was walking one afternoon on a beach when she noticed a kindly looking man strolling along and ran up to him and slipped her hand into his. They walked along together for a time. And when they had to part and go their separate ways, the man said, "Little girl, in case your mother has been worrying about you, just tell her when you get home that you have been walking on the beach today with Oliver Wendell Holmes."

That did not impress the little girl very much. She thought for a moment and then volunteered, "Well, mister, if anybody should have been worrying about you, you just say that you have been walking with Mary Elizabeth Brown."

Adults can well emulate the utter naturalness of children with either God or man. God would have us slip into His presence just as naturally and easily as a child goes to mother and father.

The key to the Kingdom is to become as a little child, just as natural and receptive and trusting. Why is it that when we grow up we make religion and faith so complicated? We can be truly happy only so long as we maintain the trust we had as little children.

A young man gave this testimony: "When I was living in a rooming house, my life was changed when I heard a seventy-two-year-old man in the room next to me get down on his knees one night and pray, 'Lord help me to be a better boy tomorrow than I was today.' At the age of seventy-two he was remembering a prayer he learned at his mother's knee."

I think of the five-year-old who said to his mother, "When I grow up, I want to be a mountain climber."

The mother wondered what fantastic idea now had gotten into his head. "Why a mountain climber?" she asked.

"Because I want to climb the highest mountain so that I can see God."

That night as the little five-year-old went to bed, he said to mother, "Mother, if I should die tonight, do you suppose some angel would meet me at the gate of Heaven and show me where to go? I am such a little boy, I might lose my way."

I thought of that when I went into a hospital room to speak to a soul at the point of death. My heart ached for this woman. She kept sobbing between periods of consciousness and unconsciousness, "Pastor, the angels have gone; the angels have gone." I tried to console her, telling her that God promised that the angels would never leave us.

I believe absolutely in angels. Not that they will always spare me the trials that come our way in a sin-blighted world. Instead, it is ever my simple faith that God's guardian angels hedge me about every moment of my life to give me power and strength to resist temptation. I believe mightily in angels, and it is horrible to think that there are lives from which God's angels have fled. God has promised never to leave His children who resist evil. Not only of Jesus, but of you, it can be written, "The devil left him, and angels came and ministered to him."

To reach the Kingdom one must become as a little child and learn to face life optimistically. Going to church leads to vibrant living. It was a favorite phrase and so often on Jesus' lips, "Be of good cheer; I have overcome the world." Jesus went about doing good. He was forever helping folks. We would be wise if we recognized that keeping ourselves busy helping needy souls will give us precious little time to be thinking of our own aches and ills.

If only we could retain the optimism of little children. When I went to grade school it seemed that it would always rain every time we were going to have a picnic. I thought of that one day when my little girl planned to go to a picnic. She was hoping that the weather would be decent, but the day dawned gray and chill, with the sun hiding behind angry clouds. Looking out the window, my little girl scanned the dark, lowering clouds. She turned and smiled at me as she said, "Daddy, I don't think it is going to rain, do you?"

I thought to myself, "How wonderful it would be if, in spite of every appearance and outward circumstance, we would look out at life and say, 'Well, I don't think it is going to happen.'" With a faith like that, come what may, we cannot be defeated.

The last column John Helmer Olson wrote for our church weekly, *The Lutheran Companion,* was from his hospital bed. The last paragraph read something like this:

A dozen beautiful red roses came into my hospital room a few days ago. Every one of them said, "We love you." For four days I have enjoyed those beautiful red roses, but now they have withered and died and I am sad. I cried to God and I said, "Why did they have to die?" And God looked upon me and replied, "It is true the roses are gone, but you did enjoy them for four days. Aren't you grateful for that?" And beyond that, if you trust, you can be sure there will always be more roses.

I am happy to be living today because life with God is to me like a walk through a beautiful garden. Some day there will even be more roses for me and for you in God's garden of Eternity. May we never lose, or never be careless with, or misplace, the key to the Kingdom!

CHAPTER XIX

THE WISE MAN

ONE DAY THE devil called his angels together. He demanded that they produce a plan to bring him more converts on earth. He observed that all too many were turning to God and embracing the Church. Frankly, he was worried. Then one of his minions stepped up to report, "My plan is to go down to earth and persuade people that there is not a Heaven." The devil shook his head. He doubted that this plan would ever work. "People never will believe that." Then a second angel of darkness asked that he be permitted to go to earth and persuade people that there wasn't any hell. "They won't believe that, either," the devil objected. Then a third fallen angel came up with a plan that won the approval of the prince of darkness. He proposed, "Let us go to earth and tell the people they shouldn't be in any hurry about their souls' welfare. Let us convince them that they can wait until tomorrow."

But time is fleeting and all too brief in which to do with what we have. Scripture reminds us that we have no permanent earthly possession, that "the earth is the Lord's and the fullness thereof." God has made us temporary stewards or overseers of the material things and talents and skills He has entrusted to us. He intends that we should use them. He asks only that we use them to help in some special way to extend His Kingdom. The day will surely come when we will be asked to give an account of our stewardship. We will be asked to show how we used the things God entrusted to us.

Luther's explanation of the first article of the Apostles' Creed reads, "I believe that God has created me and all that exists, that He has given and still preserves to me my body and soul, my limbs and all my senses, my reason and all the faculties of my mind." These words call to mind the mighty mountains that God lifted out of the earth, the beautiful rivers and lakes, the multitudinous seas with which He has covered the face of the earth. Consider the trees, the flowers, and the birds of the air, and the animals of the field. Everything that the eye beholds in this home given us to dwell in is the work of God's hand. Truthfully, now, have you stopped to thank Him for what He has done? When, to top all this, we add our minds and the capacity to think clearly, has our gratitude been enough? Think of it, thirteen thousand people in our state (Minnesota) alone are this moment patients in hospitals for the mentally ill. What a gift is sight! Think if we could never see the beauty in a child's uplifted face? Yet thousands have never seen that. They have been denied what is almost like life to most of us. Should we not join the psalmist in saying, "Bless the Lord, O my soul: and all that is within me, bless his holy name"?

Besides all this beauty, God provides us daily with the necessities of life. The average American family throws away every day more food than the average family in some parts of Asia will have to eat in an entire day.

Probably we had better revise this—more than they will have to eat in an entire week!

From behind the Iron Curtain in East Berlin recently streamed thousands of people. At the risk of their very lives they passed through the Iron Curtain and formed long lines to get their little handout of rationed food. The Communists' direst threats could not restrain them. These long lines of hungry people asked for just one thing— food. A Godless Communism can never provide people their real needs. The Communist leaders are not concerned for the individual. Their empty promises mean empty stomachs. More tragic than this is that their militant godlessness spells empty hearts. No civilization can long endure without God.

A visitor from India was touring the northern part of our country with an American social worker. One day they bought a watermelon along the way. It was so big they couldn't finish it. The American social worker made as if to throw it out the window. "Don't do that!" pleaded the Indian. "Instead let us set it by the side of the road. Some hungry people might come along and then they will have something to eat." Wishing not to offend the visitor, the American set the unused watermelon by the side of the road. They went on. After three days, when they were returning the same way, they found the watermelon still there by the side of the road. Not even the birds in this land of bounty had touched it.

"I believe that Jesus Christ has redeemed me," continues Luther in his little gem explaining the Apostles' Creed. This time he opens the second article of the Creed to our understanding. The redemption that Jesus brings is the greatest hope that life can hold for you and me.

He tells us that whatever betides, we do not walk alone. When we awaken in the morning God is with us. He promises to be guardian and guide during the day and every day to the end of the journey. The beautiful fellowship we enjoy with Christians along the way means so much. What more can we want? Wise is the man who today hears the voice of God and rises up to follow Him.

To each of us God entrusts certain things. Some of us are careless with our trust. We take our ease as if we would never be called on to give an accounting. What fools! No one of us knows the hour when God will call us to come before Him for a reckoning. Should not this cause us to stop and think what will be our lot if we fail to give God the control of our lives? I say it with deep feeling: Hell is not something that may happen to us only in the future. Hell is a present reality to him who separates himself from God. By the same logic it follows that Heaven is not a distant prospect toward which we journey. For him who lives in daily union with God through Jesus Christ his Son Heaven is a daily experience. I love Roland Hill's lines: "Jesus in the heart, the heart in Heaven, and Heaven in the heart!" We will never know life's glory until we open the gates of our heart and let Jesus in.

Who, then, is the wise man? Jesus likened him to the merchant, who finding a pearl of great price, sold everything to possess it. The wise man is he who sets his heart on "pearls of great price." "Set not your affection on the things that are below the things that are above."

If in this mad race to accumulate things we leave God out, we will lose everything. God says so in His word: "What shall it profit a man, if he shall gain the whole world, and lose his own soul?" The closer to God we are, the more will peace and happiness be ours. A baker never expects to get a better cake than the ingredients he puts in it. Yet there are people who complain that life is not what they expected it would be. They forget that in leaving out God they have left out that which alone gives life its glory, and hope, and love and laughter.

The wise man not only sets his affections on the things which are above, he busies himself with specific and worth-while things to do. God expects us to work right where we are today. We cannot excuse ourselves by saying that He gave to others greater opportunities and larger gifts. In His planning, God made each of us to fill a certain niche. If we fail Him we will leave forever undone what He put us in this world to do. One day when St. Francis of Assisi was hoeing his garden a man asked him, "If you knew you were going to die tonight what would you do?" St. Francis' simple answer was, "I would just keep on hoeing in my garden." An oil station attendant is called upon by God to be the very best attendant he can be. Whether your work is in a kitchen or a classroom or an office, God asks only that you do your best right there. This is your high and holy calling.

Again, who is the wise man? The wise man is he who has a hope worth waiting for. John Dewey, the renowned philosopher, was talking with an agnostic one day. The agnostic asked the great teacher, "Mr. Dewey, what is the good of all your philosophy? What good can it do anyone?"

"It gives me the capacity to climb mountains," replied Dewey.

The agnostic laughed and went on to say, "Well, what good is climbing mountains?"

Retorted John Dewey, "When I no longer want to climb mountains to see other mountains to climb, then life is over for me."

A Christian's trail leads to the mountain top. He can never be content to stay in the lowlands. Depression and doubt are only mists, through which God leads us up to Tranfiguration Peak, from where we can take in the vistas of glory. Tell me why do so many people give the appearance of having cashed in everything to make a down payment on a cemetery lot rather than a first payment on the House of Many Mansions?

Laugh, love, and lift, and you will live a well-balanced life. Wise is the man who can laugh. We all need more of joy. Most of us appear to be riding in wagons without any springs, feeling every bump and shock on the way. A good laugh acts like a tonic. Let us love and laugh and know the "glorious liberty of the children of God." Once I visited a woman who was in an oxygen tent. For a moment she lifted the hood enough for me to see her smile as she jested, "Pastor, I am chained to a tank!" "No, you are not chained," I said as I sensed her indomitable spirit. "You have a freedom the like of which I haven't seen in a long time." I don't know when I have been so ashamed of myself as when I left that bedside. Since then, for me to complain about the little irritations of life has seemed very, very silly.

Love! This hard-boiled world of ours is very short on love. Let us love more and lift harder. If we invest our lives in others we will not have time to let our minds dwell on our own problems. Norman Vincent Peale attests to this. A crippled man had sat for years in a wheel chair. One day he was on the beach watching his sixteen-year-old son swim. The boy ventured beyond his depth. Either because he became frightened, or was seized by a stomach cramp, the boy began to sink. Utterly horrified, and spurred by the knowledge that he was the only one close at hand, the father leaped from his wheel chair into the water and saved his son. Of course, the "cripple" has never sat in a wheel chair since. We do not mean that everybody in a wheel chair has unused and hidden strength that could be summoned to release him from invalidism. Yet I believe that there are people in mental wheel chairs playing the role of a cripple all because they lack faith. Hope is a broken string in the harp of life. "All power in heaven and on earth is given unto me," says Jesus. Is He not Creator and Redeemer, the ever-present Sanctifier of our hearts? When our faith draws a circle and brings Him in, we are wiser than all the sages of history. Sir Walter Raleigh has just the right concluding word for us:

> Give me my scallop-shell of quiet,
> My staff of faith to walk upon,
> My script of joy,
> Immortal Diet, my bottle of salvation,
> My gown of glory, hope's true gage,
> And thus I'll take my pilgrimage.

CHAPTER XX

AN INVITATION ADDRESSED TO YOU

THERE WAS A knock at the door. I opened it to a man dressed in uniform. He was holding a beautiful silver plate, on which was an engraved invitation from Prime Minister Nehru requesting our presence at lunch in the gardens of Cecil House at Delhi, India. It was an unforgettable occasion. I thought then, "Liveried message-bearer of a prime minister, I have a far greater privilege each Sunday when I stand before my people as an ambassador of Christ the King to extend an invitation to each one personally and to announce that the banquet feast is made ready and prepared by One who knows your needs." Let me repeat that invitation, "Come, for all things are now ready."

May I suggest, first of all, that everyone is invited to participate in the blessings of the Kingdom of God. But pity it is that so frequently, with our noses in the air, we pass by and spurn the spiritual banquet tables with their spread of heavenly benefits, and, instead, run greedily to the tables heavy with worldly luxuries.

Witness these happenings in contemporary life! An ice cream company advertised for some boys to be ice-cream testers. Immediately they had 2000 applicants. That boyishness persists in us grown-ups, too.

Not long ago our newspapers related that several men of our community had struck oil in Oklahoma. One well alone was said to be worth four million dollars. It was on the lips of so many men downtown the next day. I heard more than one wish he had been lucky enough to uncover that well and the four million dollars that went with it. As if money or things make up the life abundant!

How mistaken can we be? Without God, none of these physical benefits would be ours. The farmers in the drought-blasted areas of our country are realizing how dependent they are on the Lord God Almighty. They know real tragedy in losing what they have because of the lack of rain, and have our sympathy and prayers.

Who can ever pay back in dollars and cents for the physical benefits that we receive every day? Martin Luther says, "All this we receive out of pure paternal goodness and mercy and love, without any merit or worthiness on our part." Beyond all of these physical benefits are the spiritual benefits, which certainly are past all measuring—God's grace for daily living, each new revelation of His glory borne in on our souls, the opportunities for serving Him sent our way. All this, and Heaven besides, is included with His personal invitation to you.

I formerly spent a good deal of the summer time at our log cabin beside one of the smaller of Minnesota's 10,000 lakes. My family and I gathered wonderful memories there. Recently we sold that place and bought a cabin on the North Shore of the great unsalted sea, Lake Superior, near our youth camp.

Once, when we were up there getting ready to open camp, I looked through our beautiful window opening out onto Lake Superior and I missed Sand Lake and our wonderful log cabin and lovable friends there. And yet, beautiful as was Sand Lake, it can hardly compare to vast Lake Superior, and its rock-bound coast. Every day this glorious lake takes on a new beauty and reflects ever varying moods.

Even the children respond to it. One morning my little daughter remarked, "Look out of the window, daddy. The lake looks so different today." One day pounding waves send great curtains of spray over our rocks. Another day the green of the lake pressed up against the blue of the sky is simply breath-taking.

And then, again, the waters can be so placid and glassy as to be without even a ripple. The children exclaim, "Look, it is still more beautiful today!"

Life is like that, too, when it is filled with God. One day is even more wonderful than the next. So will it seem until the final moment when we shall experience that which "eye hath not seen and which ear hath not heard; neither hath entered into the hearts of men the things which God hath prepared for us." When we walk through the valley of the shadows we shall not be afraid. For we shall hear His voice bidding, "Come; for all things are now ready," and we shall know that death is not the light going out but the lantern being put out because dawn is come.

Though all are bidden, some reject the invitation. Why and how they can is so hard for me to understand. Perhaps there are some here today who have not accepted God's offer.

Someone has said that excuses are the cradles in which Satan lulls to sleep the children of men. From the very beginning of time men have made excuses. Ever since the Garden of Eden, when Adam charged the woman with his fall, men have been shifting the blame. And every time that we have excused ourselves from going God's way we have faced tragedy and defeat at journey's end.

Let us look at some typical excuses which our Lord put in the mouths of the characters in His parable of the wedding feast. "Come; for all things are now ready," so read the invitation. But one man said glibly, "No, I cannot possibly come to the feast. I have just bought some land and have to go and look it over." Either the man was a liar or he was just stupid. No real business man would buy land sight unseen. Furthermore, it was toward evening and supper time. No man in his right senses would go to look at the land by night. It was an excuse pure and simple. The man was just too busy with his own affairs.

How frequently we hear those words: "I am too busy to go to church. I have too many pressing things to take care of to bother with church affairs now. I will wait until some more convenient time to get religion and become acquainted with God." Is not this reaction exactly like that of the man they tell of who was out in a boat? The oars are beside him, but he is absorbed in a book. The boat is drifting down the rapids. Now it is headed toward the falls. Someone shouts a warning from shore, even as I now call to you as Christ's ambassador, saying, "You are headed for the rapids unless you let the Master help you pull at those oars." Will the man just keep on reading his book, or you continue in these mortal concerns having to do only with your own selfish self until doom is upon you?

The second man said, "I cannot come. I've bought five yoke of oxen and naturally I want to try them." If he really meant it, he, too, shows himself to be a poor business man. Who would buy oxen without knowing their worth? His answer was merely an excuse. He could well try his yoke of oxen tomorrow if he wished to attend the wedding feast.

The third man said, "I cannot come because I am newly married." Well, I do enough counseling to know that one of the difficulties of our age is the fact that all too many men are too busy to take their wives out to dinner. Now here would have been a good chance for our friend of Jesus' parable to take his wife out to dinner. So his was a very flimsy excuse indeed. Imagine it, "I am just married, and therefore I cannot come."

I thought of this incident when I read of a man who had stayed at a certain boardinghouse for several weeks. He noticed that one of the boarders always carried away a bucket of food from the table. Our friend assumed that this man was taking the food to his wife, who, perhaps, was sick. So one day he said, "How is your wife feeling?"

"My wife is feeling all right," replied our man of the bucket, rather resentful of the stranger's concern.

"Excuse me for asking, but I've noticed that you have carried supper to her every night this week. I suppose, then, it is because it has been so hot that she hasn't cared to cook."

The man retorted indignantly, "'Taint this week and 'taint the weather."

"Well, what is the matter then?"

"Well, my wife just doesn't like to cook and for thirty-one years I have been carrying Amy her meals."

Said the stranger, "Couldn't Amy come up and have dinner with you here some times?"

"Nope," replied the man with a note of finality, "Amy doesn't care about walking either."

Amy is a good example of the inertia of some people when it comes to spiritual things. They find so many excuses for side-stepping God's banquet of grace and their part in His Kingdom purposes.

I would be remiss unless I gave at least one good reason why each of us should accept the invitation. I give you my personal witness that when you walk with the Master on glory road life is incomparably wonderful. Any other way of life is as dull as dog days in comparison. "Come; for all things are now ready." The privilege of beginning this life is open to everyone. Who accepts the Lord's invitation?

Now could be your moment for decision. While you are sitting in a boat on the lake with a fishpole in your hand could be the moment for decision. While you are walking through the woods and listening to the birds preach a sermon to you could be the time of decision. Or while you watch a glorious sunset. Or it could be that moment in the hospital corridor when you hear, "It's a boy!" But the best moment of all is this golden now.

The Orientals have a legend of a man who sat a thousand years waiting for the gates of Eternity to open. For one moment only he allowed his tired eyes to close in sleep. In that moment the glory gates opened and shut again forever. The man had lost his moment. There come a time and place in life when we must decide which way our soul shall go, or the decision is made forever by our very indecision. Jesus' invitation is on a place card bearing your name.

I stood outside the Jaffa Gate near Mount Zion in Jerusalem. A water shed with a slight ridge rises there. So when rain comes down the water hesitates momentarily.

153

It doesn't know which way to go until the wind starts to blow. If the wind blows west, the water goes into the beautiful valley of Sharon, the valley of roses. If the wind blows east, the water flows on until at last it reaches the Dead Sea. The one way leads it to the brackish waters of living death. Going the other way it has the wonderful glory of giving the beauty of roses to a barren land. So is the forking of the ways from this worship service. It can be beauty or ashes. Life is too complex and too full of problems for anyone to try to go it alone. That you are here today tells me that you are already aware of this.

May I give you a word of assurance by relating an incident that took place in the North Atlantic? A terrible storm arose and tossed the big ship about as if it were a little toy boat.

The passengers gathered in the stateroom. Intermittently, they wept hysterically or trustfully prayed to God. When they were nearly in a panic, the weatherbeaten captain stood at the doorway. Instantly they became calm. The captain walked to the middle of the room and said, "I've sailed the seas for years, and crossed the Atlantic times without number. I know my boat. It is thoroughly seaworthy. I am here to tell you I shall do my best. I trust my boat and crew. But, above all, I have faith in God. I know that He will see us through." After one long look into the captain's face, the passengers were reassured.

I think the time has come when we need to take a long look into our Captain's face. He has traveled this way before. Look full into that wonderful face and get for yourself the absolute assurance that He has the power to lead us safely over life's tempestuous sea to the harbor on the other side.

So here is the invitation that is addressed to you. Will you accept it? If only you would listen, you would hear Him speak these words: "My peace I give unto you." And immediately a great calm would come over your soul.

CHAPTER XXI

WHERE WOULD YOU GO?

JUDAS DID NOT sell the Lord for thirty pieces of silver. Instead Judas sold himself for thirty pieces of silver and charged too much. Judas went out and took his life because with Jesus crucified, there was no living for him now. Nor is there any good reason left for living to anybody else who cut himself off from God.

But Judas is not the only guilty one. Others walked and talked with God during His sojourn on earth, saw Him perform His wonderful miracles, watched Him even transform a few loaves and fishes into enough food to feed thousands of people. And yet they made no effective outcry at the miscarriage of justice. Their indifference lumped them with guilty Judas.

As Judas planted that poison kiss on the Master's lips and the guard took Him captive on this prearranged signal Scriptures say, "All the disciples forsook him and fled." That statement captured my attention and started me thinking, "Just where would a person go if he did not have God? What would he do?" He could go along with those who say, "There is no God" or "I do not believe in God." "And what would that mean?" I asked myself.

If there were no God, there would be no immortality,

no resurrection. Something deep within us cries out, "There must be an eternity!" There is that something within us beyond the granite promises of God's Word that attests to God's master plan and enables us to face life with all its problems. We know that the best that life in this world can offer is incomparable to what God has in store for His children.

Where would we go if we did not have God? I recently entered a home where a woman lay sick. She had suffered for many months. She was a Christian woman, but still she was puzzled. "Pastor, have I done something wrong that has brought about this terrible sickness?" she asked. I answered that it is impossible to say why a specific illness comes. Suffice it to say that God does not cause illness like this woman's to happen. I have seen some of the worst reprobates apparently get the best breaks in life and some of the greatest saints suffer most. If one could not believe in God and eternity, how could anyone possibly endure an experience like this woman's?

Where can we go? It is just as bad to turn one's back on the Church. The growing feeling among people that they can get along without the Church is stark tragedy. Some people say, "Why do I need the Church? I can worship by myself as I go fishing or hunting. I can sit in my chair at home and listen to the radio." Of course. But suppose everybody decided to do that? If we disbanded the Church who would administer the sacraments? What hand would pour on us the water of life which is baptism, and which washes away the guilt of original sin? Who would preside at the Lord's Table, where we receive the assurance of the forgiveness of sin? Where would we get that inner buttressing and corporate strength that is

157

imparted through the worship in a church? To church come people of all ranks, of all economic levels, of every color, to say, "We are one in Christ!" Build a fire and almost at once the glowing coals form into a mass, giving out heat and cheer. Separate those coals; put them by themselves on the hearth, and see how quickly they become cold and die.

Most of us are agreed that there are too many denominations and divisions in the Christian Church. It was my privilege to participate in a National Preaching and Teaching Mission in the Midwest, where I had a revelation of how lay people are taking hold of evangelism. With our world on fire, they realize that every one of us must help stamp it out. They know intuitively that only as we give ourselves in greater consecration can we save the world.

Twelve thousand lay people gave practical demonstration of this by banding together to visit ninety-four per cent of the homes in an area around Indianapolis to seek out the unchurched. Six ministers of the National Council of Churches of America were brought in. We left busy parishes to come and help reach into every area of life, home, high school, college, service club. We preached from morning to night, seeking to bring the Gospel message and to back the work the laymen were doing. Our team gathered each morning at breakfast. One morning the leader suggested that we kneel down by our chairs and pray. Black and white, almost every denomination was represented, all bound together by a common faith in Jesus Christ as Saviour. As I thought of our total strength I wondered, "Why do we spend our time bickering about denominational differences while the world is being destroyed about us? We have the will to save it, and back of us is God."

Is it peace we want? Then there is only one place to go. It is to fall in with our Master. Instead of forsaking Him and fleeing, let us turn and face the battle of life with Him at our side. When we forsake God things begin to happen *to* us. When we stay with God things happen *for* us. God is not just a blind force outside our lives. He is a tremendous personal power within our lives.

I would like to share with you a tested method. Here is something to live by, something that will give meaning to each day of your lives. Every day every one of us faces grave problems and temptations to which membership in the Christian Church does not make us immune. Here, then, are four things to do: first, call up your happiest memories. I shall always be deeply inspired whenever I think on a certain incident at our youth camp in northern Minnesota. I was leading an evening meditation. God decided to preach from His heaven a sermon without words. The moon came up in its golden glory and shed its silver luster across the lake and into the eyes and faces of the children in my audience. In that silence God preached. All of you have had such moments, have heard God speaking to your soul.

Now, second, imagine yourself on a storm-tossed lake. Those sudden upsets in life when we get tense and worried are so like that. Waves threaten your boat. But then the presence of the Master becomes real, and He says, "Peace, be still." The waves are rebuked, and subside into perfect calm.

Third, choose a key word with meaning. Think, for instance, of the word "unconquerable." When temptation

159

comes think of God and say to yourself, "God and I are unconquerable!" Say it aloud, if that helps—"Unconquerable!" Or the word "everlasting." We are not just children of today; we are citizens of eternity. In your weakness think of God and consider His almighty *power*.

Fourth (and this advice comes from a doctor), when you get nervous and tense, pray to God. Say simply, "All right, God, I am getting all tense and nervous now. Please help me to calm down." It has always been my experience that God gives healing every time.

I cannot sell you my religion, because religion simply cannot be sold. It is a free gift. You either take or leave a gift. Each of us determines which way our soul shall go. I can speak only out of my personal experience of what God is like and of His help in time of need.

Once a little boy playing with his toys pushed them suddenly aside and ran into the kitchen, where his mother was busy preparing a meal. He threw his arms around her and said, "Mother, I love you!" The mother stopped what she was doing and returned the caress, saying, "Thank you, son." After the boy had gone out to play in the sandbox, a visiting friend said, "Your 'thank you' was a rather strange response to your boy's, 'I love you.'" Answered the mother, "I don't think so. If someone came and gave me a material gift I would certainly be ungrateful if I didn't say, 'Thank you.' And the greatest gift my children can give me is their love. Why, then, shouldn't I thank them for it?"

What does the love of God mean to us? Should we not thank Him by our very living? There stands One before us today who says, "My child, I love you with a love that will never let you go." All that He asks of us in return is our grateful living. "Before us is a future, all unknown, a path untrod; beside us a friend, well-known and loved. That friend is God."

May we slip our hands in His as we walk in the days ahead.

CHAPTER XXII

TAKE TIME OUT TO TAKE

ETERNITY IN

A CARCASS WAS floating down the Niagara gorge with an eagle perched on it. Tearing at the flesh with talon and beak, he seemed oblivious to the thunder of the approaching falls. Now the telltale water literally boiled about this strange raft. Still the eagle kept on eating. No doubt it thought, "I have powerful wings. Even at the brink all I will need do will be to flap my wings and be away. Till then I propose to enjoy this feast to the full." At the roaring lip of the falls the eagle spread his mighty pinions. But he could not move! His feet were frozen fast to the carcass. And so he was carried over the falls to his doom.

Jesus' word: "Walk while you have the light, lest the darkness overtake you," means to me simply this: "Take time out to take eternity in." The very best investment we can make of ourselves is to give our hearts to God. Nominal church members bow God out to the shadowy fringes of living. But with God at the heart we can know already the equality of eternal life. Be sure of this, the world cannot give nor yet take away that kind of life. Wise is the man who concentrates on the eternal and pushes lesser things to the periphery. It is supremely important to take eternity into our lives, because, both as individuals and as a world, we need desperately what Jesus Christ can offer.

Our world is in the throes of a titanic struggle. Simple arithmetic will tell you that the banner of the sickle and the hammer is gaining ground faster than the flag of the Cross on its field of blue and white.

On many mission fields we are busy at work building church compounds, which our faith requires us to do. But I am overwhelmed by the feeling that in a fast-moving battle of ideas, this is far too slow and is hardly a strategic use of money. But this I know: every time we give a gift of love to feed some hungry child across the seas we build a church. Every time we give usable clothing to someone naked, or send medical missionaries and medicines to heal the sick and bind up their sores, we are building the church. Only so can the steeples with their crosses be raised faster than the forces of evil can nail up their blood-red banners of empty hopes. And for this to happen we must get our eyes fixed on what are life's real values.

In life's great department store we so often get our price tags mixed. In my travels I find it is fascinating to compare values. In Madrid, Spain, for example, I took a cab from my hotel to the American Embassy, a distance of about two miles. The fare amounted to only twelve cents. Afterward I stopped to purchase a package of gum. It cost me thirty-five cents in American money.

Just so, spiritually speaking, we get our values twisted. We pay far too much for the inconsequential. But remembering that we go only once to life's department store, we cannot afford to mix our price tags. We need to become "God-conscious," to spend more time with His Word and to make regular use of the privilege of prayer. We need to take God into partnership in our business.

Most of us are so good at mouthing our faith but so very poor at practicing it. Accordingly, we are not as rich as we might be in the coin of the soul. Two little children with threadbare coats rapped at the door of a humble little home. Cold and hungry, they asked, "Can you give us something to eat?" The busy housewife, unwilling to let a tight schedule of supper preparations interfere, invited them in. Quickly she had steaming cups of cocoa and cookies in their hands. But one of the children, a girl, was so intent on the cup and saucer that the nourishing food set before her was unnoticed. Presently she held up the cup and, looking at the woman, asked, "Are you rich?"

The woman, glancing at her shabby slip covers and worn carpet, replied, "Of course not, my dear. We are not rich at all."

"But look," said the girl, "your cup and saucer match!"

Your cup and saucer match! The remark echoed in the housewife's mind. Long after the children were gone she mused on it and inwardly commented while setting the supper table, "Here I am with cups and saucers to match. No, not a big house, but a roof overhead, and a loving husband who soon will be home to romp with our children. Yes, and plenty of food, too! Oh, God, how rich I really am!"

To take time out for recognizing God's goodness is to spend it well. How rich we could all be if we would take eternity in and invite God into the heart from out there on life's chilly fringes. And, besides, we would live God-controlled lives.

A little boy often came late to mission school. His red eyes and tear-streaked face showed at a glance that he had been crying. "Why do you cry and why are you so often late?" asked the teacher.

"My mother doesn't want me to come to this mission school! She doesn't want me to listen to my Jesus-loving teacher. Instead, she wants me to pray to bulls and cows. She hates your God. And when I say, 'I want to go,' she only answers, 'You cannot go!' Then she whips me until I cry. But still I want to come. Then finally she says, 'All right, get out of this house and go.' And she does this every morning."

Then a smile broke through the tears as with a grateful look at the missionary the boy said, "But it is worth it!"

The lad instinctively recognized the love of God when he found it there among God's people. It satisfied him far more than ever could a pagan mother's heartless care.

The Taj Mahal is reputed to be the world's most beautiful building. Built by a mogul emperor in memory of his favorite wife, it is constructed of purest white marble. It costs twenty million dollars and took twenty years to build. Yet this exquisite marble temple is an island in a sea of dire hunger and unspeakable human need. The builder hired the world's best architects, only to put them to death on the day of the Taj Mahal's completion so that its secrets might never be copied. He wanted that palace to stand forever unsurpassed.

What a contrast is another place, also dedicated to an "undying love." Calvary's rugged slope speaks of a love so great as to be unsurpassed in the whole sweep of time.

Its cost cannot be measured, for it was the life of God's only Son. No mere human has even approached His greatness. The old rugged cross still stands out on the world's skyline inviting us to take time out to take eternity in.

CHAPTER XXIII

THE TRANSFORMING TOUCH

THE OTHER DAY I was thinking of my first radio set. To make it I took an empty oatmeal box and wound lengths of wire about it. Then clamping a set of earphones to my ears, I patiently twisted the little needle until I got the right place on the crystal. Then wonder of wonders came to me through the air. Never will I forget the marvel of it all.

Since that time we have seen the amazing evolution of this simple contraption until now colored pictures float on ether waves right into our parlors. Have you ever stopped to wonder while you were watching television how this can possibly be, and pinched yourself and asked, "Is it really me that am alive and enjoying this remarkable age?"

There are two great centuries among all the others that I would choose to live in, were such a choice open to me. My first choice would be to have lived in the first century; my second, in the twentieth. I love talking to young folks, for they so readily take to an optimist's philosophy of life. They give me real hope for the future. So often have I heard people say wistfully, "If only we could have the good old days back again." I sent one of my researchers to the library to look up in back magazines living conditions from 1910 to 1914. She reported that one company proudly boasted that it was manufacturing twenty-one brands of soup at ten cents a can; that a five-room cottage, a forerunner of our prefabricated houses, was offered for about $389. If your family needed still more room, a ten-room house was priced at $700 to $800. Those prices were unbelievable, considering price levels today. Moreover, the researcher dug out of "positions offered" that the salary of a professional man of average ability in 1914 was only $75 a month. But what were the conveniences then? Was life actually any happier then than it is today?

If grandma or grandpa or mother and dad could suddenly have stepped into today's living and had our salary scale and modern conveniences, wouldn't they have thought how wonderful it was to live in our century? Before we complain too much about our days we ought to take inventory, and, instead, thank God for all the tremendous advances that have made our lives so comfortable and enjoyable.

If we could peer into the crystal ball and see the future I am certain we would have to conclude by evidence already at hand that we have seen very little. In a day right around the corner we will go by jet plane from New York to San Francisco in two hours. If you have the money, you will be able to make a weekend trip to Africa. We will be living in a day with escalator sidewalks so that all we will need do is to step out and merely by standing still get to the corner without bending leg muscle. All this is on the drawing boards already. We are told that it is even conceivable that voices out of the past will be recalled. For the sound waves these voices set in motion still vibrate out there in space. I get alarmed at the suggestion that I might some day have to sit down and hear some of my old sermons played back. That would be purgatory for me. But, seriously speaking, think of what would happen if you could sit down and hear Abraham Lincoln giving his Gettysburg Address, or George Washington praying in Valley Forge's snow, or even the Master preaching the Sermon on the Mount!

But we are not limited to imagining the Master's voice. The Gospel I read is just as real as if Jesus were speaking it today. Is it not called "The Living Word"? The Holy Spirit operating through it makes it living and active. Moreover, Jesus promised us that He would send the Comforter, who "would take of what is mine and declare it to you." If only we will listen we won't need machines to bring God's voice to us. Our trouble is that we let other sounds stop up our ears. We let ourselves get too busy even to listen. But if we would be "still and know God" we could hear deep within His voice speaking in clear and certain tones. God promises us His Holy Spirit to work His transforming touch within us. Let us ever remember that without His work and our yielding our souls to Him there would remain a "sonic barrier" that even God Almighty cannot pass.

Says my Bible: "Man is wonderfully and fearfully made." Your body is a wonderful mechanism. It has a heart that in twenty-four hours beats 103,689 times. The blood coursing in your veins travels 168,000,000 miles in twenty-four hours. You breathe 23,240 times, and you consume on an average of three and one half pounds of food a day. You turn over in your sleep twenty-five to thirty-five times every night. You speak on an average 4800 words a day. You exercise 7,000,000 brain cells. You are simply wonderful in body alone! But think also of the soul, with its capacity for living forever, yes, and for living even now "the more abundant life." What a tremendous person you are. And yet you are only an empty blank until you allow the Holy Spirit to come in and transform and ennoble your life.

A great favorite with me is the Michelangelo story in which someone shoves a waste block of marble aside as useless. Michelangelo says, "Bring it into my studio. An angel is imprisoned in that marble and I intend to set it free." God would say of your life, "Give it to me. An angel is imprisoned within you and I desire to set it free." That, in a few words, is what the transforming touch of God's Holy Spirit will do for your life.

First of all, the Holy Spirit is God's searchlight exposing your weaknesses and sins. Are you willing to admit them to God? You will never be helped out of your sin unless you are willing to confess that you have done wrong, and seek His grace to go a better way.

Second, He redeems us. Someone has observed that it would hardly do us any good to know what people think of us, because we would not believe it. But for the sake of our eternal souls we had better believe what God thinks of us. And when He shows us where we are wrong we ought to face up to it and admit it. Scripture declares that we have no innate powers with which to correct and change our ways. But God tells me, "I can take your life and redeem it." Now, what does redemption mean? I take a battered silver cup to the silversmith. I lay it on his counter, saying, "Repair it and make it like new again."

The silversmith melts it down even as God sometimes has to melt us down. Then by his process of redemption the silversmith fashions the cup once again to a thing of chaste beauty. Just so I take my battered life to God. He redeems that life, and by His wonder-working power will make it over again.

And then, third, He renews our strength so that we have the power to soar like an eagle. This power He renews daily, so that life becomes wonderful to us. I like the philosophy of the old woman who said, "I don't think life is too difficult. All you have to do is play enough so that you don't work all the time and work enough so that you don't play all the time, and then behave during the day so that when you go to bed at night you need not be ashamed of yourself." God helps you live just that way by His marvelous and divine renewing process. He gives you the capacity really to live.

I would emphasize this truth through the examples of people who have experienced it. Listen to this testimony of a hard-boiled Ohio newspaper editor. Cancer struck his wife at the age of fifty-six. Our editor made a pact with his wife that when the suffering got too intense for her to bear any more he would end it. She was to let him know when that point was reached. Now, let him finish his powerful story as reported in an editorial he wrote: "I went to the hospital one day when she was suffering terribly. But there was something different about her. She quietly said to me, 'George, this is it.'" He said, "'I am ready to keep my promise,' and I really was prepared. I could see nothing wrong with it." But she said, "Wait, darling, I want to tell you something." Then he went on to make this testimony: "I want to tell you that I saw there in that hospital a miracle of grace. It changed my whole philosophy of life and brought to me the peace that passeth all understanding.

"No, I didn't do away with my wife. And now I see that I never could have done it. Something wonderful happened. The end of her life became a living witness to God's power to master any circumstance and make it be to the praise of His glory. Day after day I sat together with my three boys at her bedside as she revealed the faith that steadied her and her ever-deepening love of God, despite her suffering. God was giving her grace for every new onrush of pain and filling her heart with trust. Moreover, she preached powerful sermons to everybody that paused by her bed. No one," concluded this newspaper man, "could ever tell me that there isn't a Power that will help you face triumphantly anything life can throw your way."

The amazing and transforming touch of the risen, victorious Saviour can be on your life, too. It happened in the first century; it is happening in the twentieth; it can happen to you.

CHAPTER XXIV

HIS CHOSEN

In ALL THE world there is nothing so tender as Jesus' farewell address found in the Gospel of John. John, who leaned close to Jesus at the Last Supper, heard and recorded it for us. Impending tragedy weighing on Jesus' heart sent forth these words of infinite love. We read the words in cold print. But just as to the eye a power line is inert, so we miss the electric impulses of Jesus' mighty, consuming love these words carried to His disciples at that supper.

John could never get over marveling at this honor which lifted up and ennobled objects once so base and undeserving. "This is love, not that we loved him, but that he first loved us and gave himself up for us." The honor Jesus' words convey makes the highest earthly honor look like wax flowers before the real.

As a "friend of the Bridegroom" I would rather wretchedly fail after trying my best to bring you and Jesus together than gloriously succeed at any other job there is. My zeal for this springs from the desire that no one miss Jesus' transforming friendship. Not all friendships are ennobling. "Amnon," David's princely son "had a friend." It is Scripture's only explanation of Amnon's dastardly incest. For at the sheep-shearing feast, Jonadab, a friend, spurred on Amnon's wild passion for his own sister Tamar. Jonadab nudged him on to the unnatural crime, saying, "Art thou not a king's son?"

Do you remember that on the night when Jesus was betrayed the postern gatekeeper pointed at Peter, saying, "Thy speech betrays thee"? I never tire of quoting T. R. Robinson's prayer, for it has just the right concluding line:

> O that my tongue might so possess
> The accents of His tenderness
> That every word I breathe might bless
> For those who mourn a word of cheer;
> A word of hope for those who fear
> And love to all men far and near.
>
> O that it might be said of me,
> "Surely thy speech betrayeth thee
> As friend of Christ of Galilee!"

Not only our lips but our lives should betray us as Jesus' chosen.

Therefore, if we as branches are to bear fruit we must be grafted onto Christ the true Vine. To me that definitely means time for private and corporate worship.

"I will have to skip it today, I am too busy." Have you ever heard that before, when it is time for family prayers, or when the inner voice urges the discipline of the Pocket Testament? Where except in turning to Jesus in prayer are we to learn the secrets of real living? He flung down the keys to unlock every one of them who said, "A man's life consisteth not in the abundance of things." And again, "That ye may have life and that more abundantly."

The world record for the one-mile race was shattered by Bannister of England, the "runner with a head on him." He made it just under four minutes. I wish someone had timed me recently in a certain depot. I made a marvelous run for a departing train. With one last agonized sprint I jumped to the lowest step. The train was moving fast! Jubilantly I exclaimed to the conductor, "Now I will make that appointment in   ." "But we are headed for   ," he replied, naming a station in the opposite direction. Life is like that! A great many people rush like mad to make life's train, and discover too late that they are headed the wrong way. Jesus unerringly points out to every seeker the track on which the train moves heavenward.

That day is well begun when the soul is washed and freshened up by personal devotions. "Already ye are clean through the word which I have spoken," is Jesus' word on the value of the quiet time. Something akin to steel enters that heart which has knelt to say, "God is my refuge and strength." That is the way to begin a day, standing on tiptoe and looking in God's window.

Another test is this: "Ye are my friends," says the Lord, "if ye do the things which I have commanded." "To obey," says the Old Testament, "is better than sacrifice." Would you be brutal and cruel to a little child? Or be soft and indulgent? A growing number of young men are being turned aside by Selective Service and tagged, "psychoneurotic." The Surgeon General's explanation of it is: "The modern trend is away from strict home discipline." To the best of our knowledge, not one Russian has been turned aside for such a lack.

Exhaustive tests prove that children are happier in homes in which obedience is expected. Disciplined Christians are God's happiest creatures. Young Americans suckled in a creed of untrammeled liberty stop and learn today Jesus' better way: "Keep my commandments, even as I have kept my Father's commandments."

The Christian way is not merely doctrine but the way of discipline. "Faith without works is dead." Unless faith is acted upon, it is dead. Your deed is your creed. You do not believe what you do not practice. A Korean girl dropped out of the Mission Learners' Class. Sought out, she answered her questioner, "But I haven't yet practiced all that I already have learned." She felt she had to master the last lesson before she tried to learn another. She was so right!

A country parson prayed, "Lord, prop us on the leanin' side." How about it, friend? Do you need propping on the side of clean thinking? "Blessed are the pure in heart." How about that tottering side tagged, "Love your enemies"? When last did you do something for the "least of these my brethren"? Have you a leaning side that needs propping? Every day each of us ought to stop and put the straight edge of God's Word against his crooked life.

Obedience keeps our world going and in one piece. One moment's disobedience by an aviator, and—crash! A pilot cannot take a "moral holiday" while in the air. God's laws operate everywhere.

A politician was urged to give up an illicit love that was destroying two homes. He twitted his pastor by quoting a general. This general was urged by an Oxford Movement convert to make absolute honesty, purity, unselfishness, the rule of his life. He had answered with

176

the jibe: "I am going to start a Cambridge Movement for absolute dishonesty, selfishness, hate and impurity." "Why, then, don't you start doing that right now?" asked the puzzled pastor of the politician. "Why are you so timid and hesitant? Why not sin, with all the stops out?"

"Oh, no," was the general's immediate answer, "it would never work!" He gave away his whole case and argument. Evil is a parasite on good. By itself it is pure self-destruction. Every dishonest man is a parasite on the honest man, every impure man on the pure. It is the disciplined who hold society together and keep order in our world. "Suffer hardship," urged St. Paul, "as good soldiers of Jesus Christ. The effeminate" (literally, the soft) "shall not inherit the kingdom." Would you be His Chosen? Then you must keep His commandments. Listen again as He speaks, "I appointed you that you should go and bear fruit and that your fruit should abide."

Again, "This is my commandment, that ye love one another." Is that a hopeless assignment? Never! At Calvary demoniac forces of sin gathered for the "kill." Divine love looked weak and beaten that Black Friday. Yet today we know that at that moment love was splendidly triumphant. On Jesus' nail-pinned hands God held out the Divine remedy for sin. "Father, forgive them," prayed Jesus, "for they know not what they do." The blood pouring from His hands, His feet, His side was Heaven's blood plasma for our hate-filled and sundered family.

The cross is an inexhaustible fountain of love. Anyone can love, be loveable. We are all drawn to the gracious; the nobly endowed, the charming. But how many of us can be kind and thankful to the warped and ugly? Let a man prove false. Let his temper flare; let him stand in our

177

way, take advantage of us, immediately our feelings toward him change. Though he had ever so tender a heart and a love that had sent him where no white man had ever gone, Robert Moffatt confessed there were times when he gave way to a loathing for the brutal and sunken minds with whom he was thrown in contact. Missionary Chalmers admitted deep distaste for the crowds who milled around him. He even complained one day of their stupid stare, of the animal heat, and fetid smells in the place where he preached. But Christ's cross, revealing the love that sent Him to die for sinners, kept constantly renewing their love and made both men great missionaries for God. That same love will strengthen our fitful love, and it will give us a happiness that nothing can lessen.

For said Jesus in John's Gospel, "I have come that your joy may be full." Let us remember that our Christian faith was born with a song, "Glory to God." The early Christians could hardly find words to express adequately the great joy which had come into their lives. "Singing and making melody in your heart to the Lord," was the way St. Paul described them at worship. People "took note of them as having been with Jesus." Do you wonder that T. R. Glover wrote of them: "They outlived, outthought and outdied their pagan contemporaries"? Truly they were beside themselves with a great joy. Why, then, are some of us so glum and gloomy in practicing our religion? The windows of Heaven have been open, but not our hearts. We have not permitted God to take complete possession of us. We lack the inner witness of the Holy Spirit. Our faith is "second-hand."

Filled with the desire that every person at a prayer meeting might recapture that "first, fine, careless rapture"

178

of the first-century Christians, an elderly deacon prayed: "O Lord, if any divine spark has been kindled at this meeting, please water that spark." His words got tangled up. But God knew what he wanted. Accept Jesus as Saviour, and, lo, the breath of God will blow on the dying embers of your faith.

"I feel as though I had swallowed sunshine," said one Christian.

"It is indecent for anyone to be so happy," said another.

A young woman witnessed in a letter the other day, "I wish all knew Christ as I now know Him. He has made my life happier. Try praying, 'Spirit of the Living God, fall now on me.'"

And look! Instead of the Divine spark being watered, let it be fed so that it will begin to glow and burst into a kindling flame.

God's Chosen feed that flame as they give larger room to the blessing of God's wonderful indwelling Spirit.

179

CHAPTER XXV

CHRIST THE HOPE OF THE WORLD

M Y LIFE JUST doesn't count!" How often do I hear that lament from people who come to my office with their problems.

When I point out all that remains to be done in this world, they admit it is true. But, like a record that is stuck, they just keep repeating, "Yes, my life just doesn't count. My life is like a raindrop in the sea; it just isn't significant. You set my meager talents up against the great needs facing our world. It is just this that makes me so depressed!" My answer to this complaint is ever the same. "No one can budge me from this truth: Any life, even the tag end of it, can be significant if only that person will give himself to God."

Whenever I am tempted to think that my life does not count, I like to remember the tremendous consequences that have come from the little acts of service of some whose record is an open book. The story of a king who decided that he was going to build a great cathedral on the hilltop overlooking his city is a great favorite with me. The king insisted on paying the whole cost of the construction of the cathedral. Day after day, wagonloads of stone were hauled up the steep hill. Myriads of workmen swarmed over the walls. Finally, after many years of labor, the cathedral was ready for dedication, paid for entirely out of the king's coffers. The cornerstone carried only the king's name, because his consuming passion was to hand that name down to posterity. He wanted it always to be on men's lips when they entered the cathedral.

The night of the dedication service the king dreamed a dream. He saw one come to the cathedral and replace the cornerstone bearing his name with another, on which was written the name of a woman of whom he had never heard. He quickly dismissed his dream. But the next evening he had the very same dream. As before, someone came and lifted out the cornerstone bearing his name and replaced it with one inscribed with the same woman's name. It aroused him, so that he sent his servant to the cathedral to make certain that the original cornerstone was still there. The servant reported that all was exactly as it had been and the king was satisfied that his dreams were only wanderings of a tired mind.

But when on a third night he dreamed the same dream again the king sent his servants out with the order, "Go out everywhere, and if you find a woman by this name bring her to my court."

The servants went out, and found a woman of the name living in a humble little hut on the very road up which each day the horses had drawn heavy wagonloads of stone. The servants brought her to the king. She was very much afraid, and trembled visibly as she stood before his majesty.

The king said to her kindly: "I have had a very strange dream," and then related it to her. Then he concluded,

"May I ask you just one question? Did you do anything at all to help build this cathedral?"

The woman, visibly shaken, turned to say, "Honored king, I saw the horses come by, pulling their heavy wagons loaded with stone. And, seeing how tired and hungry they were, I fed them a little wisp of hay, only a little wisp of hay."

The king was so impressed by this woman who had sought to do her little part to help build the cathedral that he ordered his name chiseled out and hers to be deeply cut in the cornerstone.

Some people's names are always in the headlines, but, so far as God's work here is concerned it does not necessarily follow that these same names head all others in God's book of life. There is something for every one of us to do, even if it be to give a weary horse "just a little wisp of hay."

Who is the greatest giver mentioned in the Bible, that is, except God and His Son? Of the hundreds who passed and cast in their offerings while Jesus watched one day in the temple, who is still remembered? Was it the big givers pouring in their shekels by the bagful? No! We remember only one, a widow who cast into the treasury her all, a fraction of a cent. What little boy was singled out by our Lord to be remembered? Not a boy from a wealthy or influential home, but one who gave his lunch of a few fish and a couple of buns to Jesus. Under his very eyes that lunch was multiplied into food enough to feed five thousand people.

Little things can be significant. And when I speak of Christ as the hope of the world I want you to know that every one of you has something to do with making Christ the hope of all the world. This is not a task reserved for church leaders or for any other type of leader. There is something for every one of us to do. Little things can be very significant. You may not have much, but what you have is enough for God to use significantly if you will but dedicate your life to Him.

Also, little things can work great harm. Yielding to little sins can even bring spiritual death on us. Sometimes the evil one whispers within, "This little thing can't hurt you." But the little thing is like a little cancer, which silently grows and grows until it ends in death.

Some pictures from our mission field brought this vividly to mind. They had to be shown rapidly, for we just couldn't bear to look on these grievously sick people in Africa for very long. The pictures underscored how much sending doctors and medicine can help, and, above all, the need for the Gospel of Jesus Christ that makes every individual sacred in God's sight. The picture of a sick tribesman was shown to us. (I had to avert my eyes. In all my travels around the world I had seen nothing so bad as this.) Half of his head was eaten away. There was an open sore bigger than my face. Of course, death was waiting for the victim.

I asked, "What happened?" The missionary said, "He had a little scratch on his head, only a little scratch to begin with. Then it became infected." How do these natives treat a little scratch that becomes infected, not having medicine? Only to relate this is revolting, but we need to be jolted out of our lethargy. Well, how do they treat it? They pick up manure from the ground and smear it over the sore. Naturally the scratch becomes infected.

And yet we in America are so slow to share our vast medical know-how with the ignorant peoples of the world.

Driving up the trail leading to Sawbill Lake in northern Minnesota you must pass through great forests of virgin timber. Suddenly you come on a great opening where the land is naked and black and silent. Ugly charred sticks are mute testimony that a devastating fire roared through the forest that once stood here. As you drive along a sign says, "This forest fire was caused by someone carelessly discarding a single lighted match." Again I thought of the tremendous damage caused by something as insignificant as a half-burned match or a cigarette butt. It is also true that great good can have small beginnings for which only one person may be really responsible. There is always something that you can do.

Shall we think, first of all, what Christ, the hope for the world, can do for you? A great change must come over you before you can effectively witness to others. There are two suggestions, among many others, I would single out. Take a long look at Thorwaldson's statue of Christ, a great favorite of mine ever since I was a little boy; in that immortal statue the bidding Christ stands with arms outstretched. The Bible verse that was in Thorwaldson's mind when he created his masterpiece was, "Come unto me, all ye that labor and are heavy laden, and I will give you rest." And our window depicts Jesus welcoming each of you to His heart and saying, "I will give you rest."

Now, if you will always keep looking up to Him you will stay out of trouble. As an example, look at Peter. He is in a boat which is threatened by a squall much like the storms that come suddenly upon us. He and the others despair of their lives, when, suddenly, Christ appears walking to them on the waves. Peter cried, "Lord, let me come over to you." And impulsively he is over the side of the boat walking to Jesus over the waters. So long as he kept looking to Jesus he was all right. Then he eyed the angry waves surging about him and became frightened, and began to sink. He shrieked, "Lord, help me or I perish." And at once Jesus' arms caught him up.

If you will keep looking to Jesus and permit Him to guide you in all things, you, too, will come safely through every trial. If you will begin each day by praying, "God, go with me as my guide; tell me in each situation what to do and what not to do," I can guarantee that your feet will not stray.

Every day at our summer camp I am wont to remind our young people, "Do this and I will never need to be concerned about you." I repeat it now to you, because, after all, are we not all little children? Every morning say, "God, please walk with me wherever I must go today." Then there will be some places you will avoid, places where you cannot take Jesus as your companion. There are certain things you will not do with Him at your side. Keep your heart door open to Him, and you will never bring shame or reproach to your loved ones. Once Jesus is permitted to take over our lives, great things begin to happen.

So look again at this stained-glass window. See the disciples clustered around the Master, who stands with outstretched arms on the Mount of Ascension. It is forty days after Easter. Jesus is about to return to Heaven and He is saying to His disciples and to us, "Go ye into all the world and make disciples of all nations, baptizing them in the name of the Father, Son and Holy Spirit."

Then He added a promise which I want you to repeat to yourselves as you leave church: "Lo, I am with you always, even unto the end of the world."

Do you realize how vastly rich we are when we have with us the King of kings and the Lord of lords? With such a faith inspiring life and outlook, it is wonderful to think of what follows in its train. Christ-possessed children and young people constitute a great hope for this world of ours. I trust that God will let me live long enough to see the investment which my church has made in its young people begin to pay off. The chain reactions that this dynamic faith sets in motion are limitless.

Sit with me through some of the nightly prayer sessions at our camp. A little nine-year-old boy who had never been up North Shore way before conversed with God as naturally as he would have talked with me. He said, "God, it was tremendous, this trip up here today. I never dreamed there could possibly be so many beautiful falls. And Lake Superior is so big!"

And he went on, "God, when I got here to Caribou Lake, I ran down to the shore. There I saw tadpoles all over, hundreds of them. No. There must have been thousands of them. I saw these little tadpoles and . . ." He waxed so enthusiastic as he talked to God. "God," he said, "I thought to myself, 'Look at those little tadpoles. Some day they are going to be great big frogs.' And, Lord, I am little, too. But help me to keep looking up so that one day I will grow to be big and fine for you."

Then an outstanding high-school athlete prayed a beautiful prayer. In portraying Christ as the world's hope I had touched on the great potential of the Christian family, how that if we really stood up and dared to be

CHRIST THE HOPE OF THE WORLD

counted, wars would never be. There would be no hungry people, or sick and homeless, since there is always enough for all in this world. After the message, this boy prayed, "Lord, help us to do our part in awakening this great, sleeping giant of Christianity so that great things will happen in our day. I want you, Lord, to know tonight that in all my life you have never let me down." Then he closed his prayer by saying, "Now, Lord, help me never to let you down!" That was all. He had put in his prayer the nub of everything I have been asking of you: Never let God down.

On a previous occasion, the same enthusiastic nine-year-old boy, on hearing rain pelting on the chapel roof, prayed, "Lord, listen to it rain! A single drop at a time doesn't matter much. But, Lord, if there are enough of them, there will be bucketsful of water. And, Lord, do you know what it all reminds me of? Well, our church. It, too, was just a little drop of water in its beginning. And now think how big it is!" And then he added, "Help me to grow that way, too."

Then he went on to preach to me one of the best sermons I have ever heard in all my life. On our camp altar are two single candles. An everlasting light stands in the center and is never snuffed out. (But at the close of the service the end candles are snuffed out, to be lit again for the next service.) The boy prayed, "Lord, as I look at that altar, here is what I think. I don't want my life to be like those two end candles when they are snuffed out. Instead, help my life to be like the center candle, an everlasting light shining for you."

No one can possibly grow to be too wise for the message of these simple childhood lines:

Jesus bids us shine with a clear, pure light,
Like a little candle burning in the night.
In this world of darkness we must shine,
You in your small corner and I in mine.